THE CONSCIENTIOUS MANAGER

Nurturing Workplace Ethics And Synergies

PHANI MEDICHARLA

ATLANTIC

PUBLISHERS & DISTRIBUTORS (P) LTD

ATLANTIC
PUBLISHERS & DISTRIBUTORS (P) LTD

7/22, Ansari Road, Darya Ganj, New Delhi
Tel.: +91-11-4077 5252, 2327 3880
E-mail: orders@atlanticbooks.com
Web: www.atlanticbooks.com

Published by Atlantic Publishers & Distributors (P) Ltd 2024

Previously Published by SAGE Publications in 2021

Printed & bound in India by Atlantic Print Services

ADVANCE PRAISE

'Conscientious' comes from the root word 'conscience', which gives a person a sense of right and wrong to guide one's behaviour. We live in challenging times which are likely to put us on horns of dilemma. *The Conscientious Manager* by Phani Medicharla comes like a breath of fresh air to refresh youngsters, learners and leaders in the context of their life. The stories speak to your heart, the examples tell you it is possible and, importantly, the questions nudge you to action. It is a delight to savour.

Emmanuel David
Director, Tata Management Training Centre;
Strategic Leader, Influencer and Coach

Phani Medicharla has written a wonderfully readable book full of wisdom which applies to business and life. The book is organized in bite-sized, memorable tales which combine our childhood love of stories with our adult desire to extract knowledge from life experience. The result is guide to interpersonal challenges and organizational dynamics in business that you won't be able to put down or forget.

Dr Tanya Menon
Professor of Management and Human Resources,
Fisher College of Business, Ohio State University

This collection of short stories is a tour de force in humanity and human interaction. Questioning our values and beliefs as well as how we interact with each other through a series of pointed tales which often holds up a mirror and forces the reader to consider their own actions is brilliantly done in the book, with subtle humour and little moralizing, taking the reader on a journey of self-discovery and learning. This is from a writer who is at the sharp end of technology, well versed in all things—artificial intelligence, automation and the next wave of information technology innovation—and yet spends a lot of time and effort on the people side of that revolution. I think he knows something we should all be aware of. Enjoy!

Jan Steenberg
FCILT, Honorary Secretary and Trustee,
Chairman of The Education Standards Committee,
The Chartered Institute of Logistics and Transport-International

The art of storytelling is to make the tale relatable to the reader. Phani Medicharla crafts these stories masterfully, ensuring that powerful themes are interwoven into enjoyable narratives, engaging the reader with endearment and connectedness to the characters. The themes are the lessons and ethics of life, of how we should treat one another whether in the business world or socially. Any manager reading this book will be better enabled to empower their team, and any member of a team reading this book will be more empowered.

Dr Raj Joshi
Expedition Leader, Adventurer, Extreme Medicine Specialist,
Patron & Advisory Board, World Extreme Medicine;
'Seven Summits' Summiteer (Highest Mountain on Every Continent);
Inspirational Speaker, Change Management Expert

In *The Conscientious Manager*, Phani Medicharla gives us timeless workplace wisdom in a very compelling manner. He masterfully leverages the art of storytelling in highlighting key workplace dilemmas and follows it up with key insights and practical suggestions. The book is relevant not only for business management but for life in general, and the format with contextual stories gently leading into more concrete learnings is both holistic and specific in an elegant combination. You will not regret reading it!

Johan Prom
Board Member, SBAB,
Ex-CEO, Avanza

Of the six Ms of management—money, machines, methods, material and minutes—the sixth M, men or people, is the most important. It is humans who give relevance to the other five Ms. This is the most important message of this book. It nudges every reader to reflect on fundamental issues connected with workplace ethics. It underscores the importance of every individual in the team and the role he/she can play in creating synergies and collaborating with fellow team members. It urges purpose-driven professionals to contribute to an inspiring work culture. And all this is conveyed through the medium of simple yet heart-warming stories. In today's stressful work life, there is need for literature that encourages members of this complex corporate ecosystem to find their true purpose at work and achieve it conscientiously. To this end, the author has made a valuable contribution.

Dr Shashank Shah
Bestselling Author of The Tata Group,
Win-Win Corporations *and* Soulful Corporations

The world is in great need for people with value-based orientation in their lives. Especially with the backdrop of advancements in artificial intelligence and technology, the need for humane direction and value-based answers is even more relevant. I hope that this book written by Phani Medicharla will be used as a guideline towards finding such value-based answers to aid daily decisions in a practical manner. I wish that the readers work through the book as a guideline following the examples and experiences shared and derive benefit for their own contexts.

Folker Mittag
Member of Initiatives of Change for Business Secretariat; Former Financial Director and General Manager in a German Multinational Firm

Phani has done an exemplary job of describing 'the conscientious manager'. He brings together his years of expertise into an interesting and readable book on the workplace dynamics and diverse issues surrounding that. As a reader, it reminds you of the challenges that you would be facing at the workplace and overcoming them.

The best part about the book is the list of actionable items that the readers can draw from. If you can actionize some of them, it will bring in a major change to the way you will be looking at your career. His stories and insights are easy to relate with and helps you revisit your memories.

A must-read for working professionals.

Dr Hory Sankar Mukerjee
Principal—Education, Training and Assessment, Infosys Limited

For a topic which excessively covers malpractice and fraud, the proactive and positive narrative of this book is fresh; it provides a guide to build the foundation of an ethical culture with conviction.

Phani's workplace insights, told through an engaging storyline, give a strong argument for being a 'conscientious manager'.

Dr Anita Shantaram
Founder, Ethics India, a Legasis Company; Head, The Compliance and Ethics Academy

Living up to the title, *The Conscientious Manager,* this book speaks to you at the level of conscience and makes you reflect on seemingly routine choices which have a profound impact on your career trajectory. Written with years of minute observations of workplace challenges, dilemmas and opportunities, it is an engaging, practical and inspiring book. *The Conscientious Manager* belongs to everyone who aspires to be a better person, colleague and leader.

Atul Mathur

Author of Writing High-quality Standard Operating Procedures *and* Break Free: A Practical Guide to Getting a New Job

To my parents and grandmother

To the child in me
and all of us

To the 'teacher' in all the
teachers that come around to
show us the way

CONTENTS

FOREWORD

I am delighted to write a foreword to this wonderful book, *The Conscientious Manager*, written by Phani Medicharla.

There is more than one reason why it is my pleasure to write this foreword. First and foremost, this is a book of stories which all of us can relate to and take to heart. I am a strong believer of the powerful, timeless art of storytelling and the positive impact it has on our lives. Hence, writing an introduction to such a book gives me great joy.

Second, Phani Medicharla is a valued colleague in the Tata Group, and I am so happy that he has taken the initiative to write this book to share his learnings and knowledge. Writing is, like storytelling, a powerful art which helps convey what we know and what we feel to the world at large. It is often a distillation of our experiences and learnings, which adds great value to the reader. I would, therefore, like to encourage many more of my Tata colleagues to develop a keen interest in writing, and Phani's book is certainly a step in that direction.

Third, this is such a thoughtfully crafted book. I have thoroughly enjoyed reading it and have no doubt that you will relish it too.

All of us have listened to stories since our childhood. This book reminds me of the beautiful stories which my mother would narrate to me—stories from Indian epics such as the Ramayana and the Mahabharata. Later, in school, I began reading stories from the *Panchatantra* and *Aesop's Fables*. Stories from the Holy Bible also moved me greatly. These stories were very interesting in their own right, but many of them also conveyed a moral—a lesson about how we should conduct our lives for our own good and that of the world around us.

Stories taught us the difference between good and evil, noble acts and shameful deeds, what makes people truly beautiful and ugly. In fact, most of our early moral lessons, throughout our schooldays, typically come from stories that we read or listen to, rather than any deep reflection about our own lives.

Many years later, in business school, stories would often be disguised as 'case studies', authored by learned professors, and we would then discuss them in detail in the classroom. Here, the lessons were sometimes not so black and white, but at the end of the discussion, we would still take home valuable lessons from them.

Phani's book takes forward this wonderful tradition of storytelling into our daily workplace, into the dilemmas which we face as we interact with our superiors, peers and team members in the pursuit of our collective and individual goals. He invites you to partake in these stories with no expectations, except to sit back and enjoy the tales. Yet by the time he has narrated an anecdote, drawn an analogy and shared a real-life experience, the learning is clearly there in front of us. We cannot miss it and, quite seamlessly, the lesson seeps into our mind.

I love the fact that these are simple stories, and what makes them even more impactful is that they are used to cast a light on commonplace workplace dilemmas and circumstances which occur in all our lives. Whether it is the importance of ownership and accountability, or dealing with naysayers, or facing challenges with persistence, or the strong need for empathy while leading people—these are by no means arcane or far-fetched situations. Each of us have inevitably come face to face with them, and we need to build our own internal compass on how to navigate through them.

The Conscientious Manager provides us a practical guide in these matters, built from Phani's real-life experiences. There is no empty theorizing here; on the other hand, there is precious wisdom born from years of dedicated work and on-the-job learning. Such wisdom is perhaps the most valuable because it is shared after deep reflection and represents the author's strongly held life beliefs.

For all these reasons, I hope you will decide to read this book, enjoy its stories and reflect upon the lessons that it endeavours to share. My congratulations to Phani Medicharla on his commendable effort and best wishes on his continued voyage of writing.

Harish Bhat, Brand Custodian, Tata Sons;
Passionate Marketer, Author and Columnist

> *After nourishment, shelter and companionship, stories are the thing we need most in the world.*
>
> Philip Pullman

Meaningful sustenance and innovation are the call of the new-age enterprises—meaningful not just for the business growth of the enterprise but also to the associates of the enterprise and the markets that they serve. And at the core of such an innovation and growth lies a conscientious individual who is driven and motivated. It is this individual, wearing the hats of a leader, researcher, medical practitioner, business analyst, field technician, front office agent or any of the plethora of roles that comprise an enterprise/endeavour, who needs to be constantly nurtured and ennobled with an excellent value system and culture of the organization. This can happen only when every individual is embraced for who they are, their latent potential is understood and their aspirations are respected.

The increase in focus across organizations to make diversity and inclusion living mantras, rise of subjects like ethics in artificial intelligence and robotics and conscious efforts to move towards sustainable endeavours in business and several such efforts in the industry point to the importance of being 'driven by ethics and values' and also seen as such.

POWER OF STORIES IN LEARNING

As most Indian children of the time, and perhaps this is a timeless phenomenon, my early education started in the lap of my grandparents and parents, listening to moral stories. My earliest impressions and foundations of the moral code of the world came from these stories. I also believe that this is the spark that ignited the engine of learning in me and gradually led to reading books on my own as a kid. 'We have exhausted the stories we know; now you should read and find your own stories,' they would say lovingly.

Years later, when I joined Little Flower Junior College in Hyderabad, I was in the class of another great storyteller in Dr E.V. Subba Rao, one of the authors of our physics textbook, who used to say, 'First you should connect with the subject, then automatically nature will reveal herself to you via these physics formulae and equations, lend me your ears…,' and talk about the great stories behind the concepts and discoveries in physics before introducing the concept itself. I was fortunate to continue to meet many great teachers throughout my formal education and then in the professional world, who employed this technique of storytelling to connect with people and enhance the quality of work done.

As I practised the art of storytelling and interacted with others who employ this art, I learnt the following:

- Stories get out of the way (of learning) and unburden the reader/listener by not imposing a direct expectation of learning.
- They take one to a different context than their own, which frees up the mind.
- This leads to the possibility of reflection and wonder (awakening the child within), which is the basis for learning.
- Indirect and suggestive nudges via characters and their conversations help the reader absorb the idea.
- The reader goes through a positive reaffirmation of known values/management principles or gets introduced to new ones gently.
- As one empathizes with the struggle or challenge of the characters of the story, it leads to strengthening of one's own

belief system and provoking the thought process to apply the principles to their individual professional context.

CONSCIENTIOUS MANAGER

Every individual is a manager of sorts. If at all there is something common across workplaces, it is 'constraints'—and we learn to deal with them from the very first day. Nobody gets to have infinite resources or time to achieve what they must. But the ones who stand out as exemplary are those who manage the constraints without ever losing out on their professional moral code. The stories in this book stem from not just my personal experience but also from the interactions and day-to-day experiences of such managers (individuals) who remain steadfast in their conscientiousness, despite constraints at multiple levels—interpersonal, organizational or external. It is these 'conscientious managers' who drive the agenda of their teams and their organization forward from day one, as they start their journey from trying to find their place, all the way up to becoming influential leaders with an inspiring reputation. And this is what you will find in these stories. The stories narrate the struggles of finding one's place, learning and sharing, leadership, interpersonal skills, culture, diversity and inclusion, letting go, enabling others, customer centricity, leading by example, organizational decision-making, reputation and others.

STRUCTURE OF EACH CHAPTER

Anecdotal Story

A conversational approach is taken for most of the stories, and the workplace morals are communicated via conversations between the characters in the story. While providing an engaging reading experience, the intent is to evoke self-reflection and encourage the reader to draw personal insights.

#WorkplaceWhispers

Here is where I have tried to draw analogies from the workplace and shared a few real-life experiences. These are common day-to-day work experiences which I am sure the reader would have personally gone through or heard from a friend at work. I have also shared the perspectives of steadfast conscientious managers I have known and worked with, which tie into the morals being discussed in the chapter. I believe that to find inspiration, we need not look far. It is found in the individuals that surround us.

#GameofDrones

While individual heroics are sometimes essential to save the day, what gets real progress in a workplace and makes it a joyful place is when things are done collectively—when there are 'synergies' at play and we can work freely with each other with mutual respect and trust.

However, there are roadblocks (also known as derailers) at multiple levels—individual, team, organizational, immediate work environment or external—some of which we can control and some we cannot. This section helps you identify those which you can control and gives you a starting line. Discovering and facing the roadblocks head-on is the first step in solving them. And you tend to unfold a synergy with another person or the environment to the extent you manage to overcome a roadblock or clear someone else's roadblock at the workplace.

So, DRONES is?

Discovering **RO**adblocks to
Nurturing **E**thics and **S**ynergies

I have avoided giving a scoring system and pushing the reader into a grading bucket (on a scale of 1–10, how bad is this problem!). Instead, let us take a more playful approach. As you discover and evaluate each roadblock, think of it as a real drone and see how it is doing. How well can you make it fly?

- **Fully autonomous flight:** You have full control on the roadblock and have managed to overcome it naturally in your workplace behaviour. Now you can appreciate the problem (that this is worth solving) and help others overcome their problems. Go help someone who is unable to fly their DRONES themselves; you are a conscientious manager as far as this DRONE is concerned.
- **Guided flight:** You recognize the need to improve, have found a friend or a mentor in the team and are able to overcome the roadblock with their help consistently (but have not fully conquered the problem, so some more work to do—keep going!).
- **Irregular flight path:** There is either lack of conviction/applicability of the roadblock or you need help to get over it. Here is where you need to focus most and get help. I have found it easy to rely on a friend at work and make repeated attempts at overcoming challenges. And as the famous quote by Nora Roberts goes, 'If you don't ask, the answer is always a "no".'
- **Unwilling to take off:** You do not empathize with any of the roadblocks listed (they don't apply to you) or you do not have any of these problems. You have two options: (a) make your own list or (b) discuss with your colleagues/friends/mentors to help you evaluate better. Chances are that you do not have this roadblock at all, and you may be in the 'autonomous flight mode' too!

Revisiting this section often, individually, jointly with your team or along with your friends at work, helps identify the progress with the roadblocks and define appropriate actions. And actions are more powerful when they are practised together with others and yield lasting results, which is what the next section is about.

#KeyResonatingActions

Here I have given the actions which I practise myself and those which I have seen being practised by successful professionals in the industry. Some of these I am sure would ring a bell with you too. As with the previous section, use this as a starting line and add your own resonating actions contextual to your environment. When the entire team resonates and lives a moral (seen as team culture) as a working principle, then it is easy to implement the behaviour and the team succeeds faster.

#StickyNoteWorthy

Quotes from notable leaders and noble humans, related to the morals or the key resonating actions, are discussed in this section.

HOW TO READ THE BOOK

At its heart, this is a book of heart-warming stories. There are no hard conventions as long as you understand the structure of each chapter, as explained in this introduction. I have the following minor suggestions to make.

- The term 'ethics' referred in this book relates to proven workplace behaviours and practices which bring people together, unlock synergies and drive common good. The attempt here is not to give a comprehensive set of all workplace ethics but to touch upon several important ones.
- I have used the words 'individual', 'associate' and 'team member' to refer to the role played by someone in their individual capacity. As an example, even the CEO of a company can have responsibilities as an individual collaborator. While the

word 'team' is used in most places to refer to one's immediate team, based on your context it may also refer to the extended supplier, vendor or partner teams.

- Similarly, the words 'lead', 'leader' and 'manager' are used to refer to the role of influencing and taking accountability of others (a team) apart from oneself.
- I have provided quotes and experiences from friends and industry experts to substantiate the point being spoken about. And unless I have explicitly mentioned it, all other narratives, although inspired by real incidents, are fictional and any resemblance to an existing entity/individual is purely coincidental.

In conclusion, and as most of the experienced readers would concur, there is tremendous interdependence, and workplace is a mesh of intricacies with huge overlaps. The intention with the narratives of the book is not to push the reader to a definitive stand, rather to engage the reader in a self-affirmative discovery of the work ethics which they uphold and make an appeal to them to apply those to their contexts in a meaningful manner in their day-to-day roles while being 'the conscientious managers'.

ACKNOWLEDGEMENTS

Attempting a book such as this on workplace morals would not have been possible without witnessing several role models within and outside the workplace who upheld highest moral principles even under tricky situations. Highlighting a few names does not do justice to the appreciation and gratitude that I have for all of you; however, I will make a bold attempt at taking a few names.

My heartfelt gratitude to Shri K. C. Narayana for introducing me to the higher levels of thinking and practice at a young age, for the continued guidance, shaping my thought process at various stages of my life and being a constant source of inspiration.

I feel privileged to receive a foreword from Harish Bhat, brand custodian, Tata Sons. I am sure that the readers will benefit from his insightful introduction to the book and his views on the subjects discussed. Special thanks to all the exemplary individuals who I have joyfully quoted in the book, you know how much you mean to me. I am very grateful to all the distinguished early readers from academia and industry who have provided their endorsements and praise.

My sincere gratitude to V. Rajanna, Senior Vice President and Business Unit Head for Technology at TCS, for always being available and for the constant encouragement and support. Thanks to K. Ananth Krishnan, Executive Vice President and Chief Technology Officer and Amit Bajaj, Corporate Vice President—Markets at TCS, for your inspiration and encouragement.

I take a bow in gratitude to Emmanuel David, Director, Tata Management Training Centre, for his continuous support and mentoring through the various phases of the book. He has been a constant source of encouragement, insight and direction.

Phani Vellanki, thank you for the unshakable faith and walking the mile along with me as I drafted the book. Thank you, Keshav Varma, for your untiring enthusiasm and pushing me to get to several start lines professionally. Without you both

I would not have gathered the momentum to start working on the book. My appreciation and special thanks to Shanker Mishra, my close ally in the day-to-day professional adventures and experiments. Special thanks and a big high-five to all my friends, colleagues and my wonderful team at TCS.

Several brilliant and compassionate individuals have helped me with their continuous feedback over the years and played a key role in shaping my skills. Jan Steenberg, thank you for your constant encouragement, astute comments and elaborate discussions on various perspectives. Thanks to my friends Nrusimha Kiran, Murali Chaturvedi, A. Srikanth, Ravishankar H., Lakshmi P. and Srilakshmi Bala Prakhya for seeing value in what I wrote early on and clapping louder than the others.

Thank you, Dr Tanya Menon and Dr Aravind Chandrasekaran from Ohio State University, Fisher College of Business for your interactions on specific topics around workplace dynamics and seeing the bright spots in my articles. Sincere thanks to Dr. D.V. R. Seshadri from the Indian School of Business for taking out time in discussing the concept of the book and giving the much-needed pat on the back during the initial phases of the book. Thanks to H. N. Shrinivas, Executive Vice President and Global Head—Human Resources (retired), Taj Hotels, and Dr P. V. Ramana Murthy, Executive Vice President and Global Head—Human Resources (retired), Indian Hotels Company Ltd, for the inspiration behind the Taj hotel story and permitting me to use the same.

This section would be incomplete without thanking Namarita Kathait from SAGE for her encouragement and feedback from the beginning and working with me in shaping the book to its current state. Thank you, Manisha Mathews from SAGE, for the early guidance and feedback. Thanks to Shruti Gupta and the entire team at SAGE for the wonderful work you have done to accentuate the content of the book and packaging it so well.

1

BEYOND THE MIST

Importance of Context

It was a seemingly dull morning in the month of June with dark clouds dominating the Stockholm sky. There was an unusual chill in the air aided by a stubborn drizzle which threatened to turn into a downpour anytime. A general sense of urgency drove every stride on the road as people tried to scurry along to reach their destinations (it was office time anyway!). Still a couple of streets away from the office, fighting with the thoughts of the umbrella lazily left behind, 'I should've taken that short blue one at least,' I tried to accelerate my pace as well.

Just to make it a bit quicker than usual, I decided to take a short cut, a path which goes from the front of a small factory leading up to the back door of the office entrance. As I took the turn to the street where this factory was located, I could see dense white fumes engulfing the front side of the factory and completely blocking out the road. And the fumes were coming out in quick bursts as if they were not going to stop anytime soon (sign of an ongoing situation!).

'Why hasn't anyone made the call to emergency services…,' I thought as I paced up faster towards the main gate. 'Or maybe they did…. In any case, shouldn't you be walking in the opposite direction, why are you getting close!' protested my mind still unable to believe the shocking sight and the counter-intuitive reaction. But hang on a bit! there were others moving along the street without the slightest concern on their faces, although it did not slow their pace (but of course all of us were in a hurry anyway to escape the impending downpour).

This definitely didn't feel right. I could not be the only person on the road concerned about the situation, 'Oh! where is this emotionless world headed, with such apathy!' I marched on nevertheless, with a quick swipe of sweat beads from my forehead. I inched closer to the gate to check if I could find a soul within the factory premises before I pressed the panic button (and for some reason, the fumes did not suffocate and discourage me from going forward!). There was nobody in there, and the fumes were coming out thick and strong from one corner of the inside premises. One foot from the gate and still clueless, as I turned around to make the call, a yellow-coloured signboard hanging on the outside of the door caught my attention (Figure 1.1).

Phew! Although relieved, that felt like a smack at my stupidity. What intense moments before the fact hidden behind the mist came to the fore. I was glad that nothing was wrong, and I did a little bit to get closer to the situation to figure out,

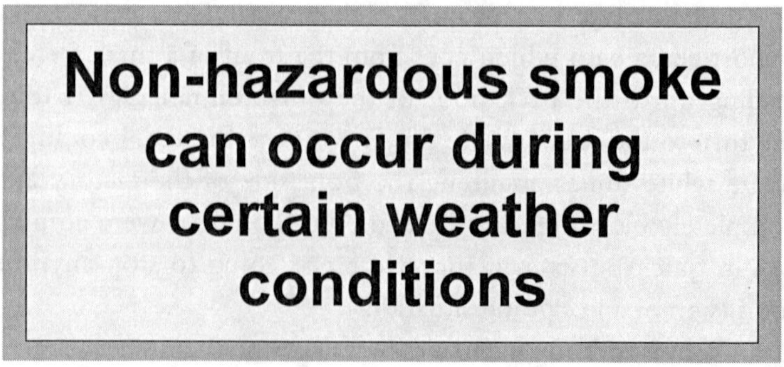

Figure 1.1 Beyond the Mist

instead of hitting the panic button. Had I dialled the emergency services, I would have looked utterly stupid.

My mind instantly threw out a silliness alert, 'Your clouded eminence! The mist is not around, but within thy head aided by a heavy dose of prejudice.' 'But hey!', I retaliated, 'It was thick, misty, dense and fuming, all signs of a hazard, eh?' Apparently not!

#WorkplaceWhispers

When was the last time you heard this phrase at work, 'What I meant with this was…?' Chances are that even you have used it not too long ago! Regardless of the role one plays in an organization, there is a part of the work life which demands 'sharing information', and it comes in several flavours—quarterly reports, management reports, status updates, progress reports, assessments, feedback, decision material, audit reports and so on. Each of these are loaded with context—some of which gets captured via data and annotations—but often than not, the rest of it remains elusive and needs to be discovered via collaboration and taking a closer look.

NOBLE TASK OF PROJECT STATUS REPORTING

I have seen seasoned professionals spending a lot of time and energy while creating information which gets shared, to prevent 'misunderstanding' on the part of the receiver. Certain organizations/teams approach it via templates and guidelines to ensure that the information capture happens in a standard format. However, it is important to enrich data/information with the right insight (signpost) every time. Just like food and medicines expire, data/information also tends to get spoilt (figuratively) with time, and adding the preservative of insight/context always helps.

How can one do this?

1. At a minimum, do not blindly send information which you don't yourself understand. This happens especially when one is being (or playing the role of) a coordinator and passing the information from one group to the other.
2. Use your experience or consult with your team to uncover perspectives which can be overlooked by busy eyes (most people consume information in a rush).
3. Ensure timeliness of sharing the information as well as the relevance of the information being shared (no one likes to receive a red alert with no time left to do something about it!).

Consider the status summary given below as a fictitious example and see how perspectives can get built up.

'We have skipped the milestone and project status is being reported as amber.'
(Clearly an indication of impending failure.)

(What if, one adds)
'This is as per earlier predictions. We are going through the most complex phase of execution, and we will be able to catch up in the subsequent sprints.'

(Even further)
'90 per cent of such global implementations across the world so far have failed, and we have come a long way in executing this programme. All our metrics indicate that we are headed in the right way.'

(And further)
'Expect the next two sprints also to be in amber status, after which we should catch up on the progress and start trending to green.'

The above construct is something I have personally witnessed several times in complex programmes. There is also another common aspect of stakeholders leaving and new ones joining the programme with minimal to no background, which adds to the confusion.

To qualify a cold fact (of missing milestone) and link it with additional and inspiring perspectives takes experience, industry exposure and right mindset. It is no wonder that certain individuals (like programme managers) are always tasked with most complex work and are trusted by customers. They tend to not just drive the programme through tough times but also keep the stakeholders engaged with a positive and supportive mindset. 'I know the programme status seems to be in red, but I will worry only when my trusted programme manager tells me so' is a common remark from senior customer stakeholders who rely on effective programme managers to steer the programme to safety.

ORGANIZATIONAL CHANGE MANAGEMENT

Another aspect where right messaging might make or break the deal is in organizational change management. Most programmes tend to succeed with technology implementations but fail with adoption—people don't like using the new tool. 'They have not considered our needs. What do they know of my daily life and they have suddenly thrown this new application and process at us?' they would say. Here as well, it is important to both personalize the communication and ensure the right timing. Helping the teams understand how a change will translate meaningfully in their daily lives and the support they will receive to implement the change allows them to participate better and not resist the change.

#GameofDrones

AS AN INDIVIDUAL SHARING INFORMATION

- In my job role, I tend to share many status reports but do not spend enough time thinking about the receiver(s) and what value these reports are adding.
- There is no set frequency of how I share information; I just broadcast it as soon as I collate data.
- I am working on complex tasks and delegate the job of conveying information and status updates to other junior associates.
- I usually find myself providing explanations to angry stakeholders on why project progress is poor; they don't understand the complexity of the work involved.
- I have been sending same communication from several months, but it just gets ignored and no one acts.
- For me, information sharing is a routine task; everybody does it and it distracts me from other important work that I do.

AS A LEADER/CONSUMER

- I get easily critical of the data/information I receive from my team.
- I do not appreciate too much detail; everything should be packaged in a small summary.
- My communication and broadcasts are direct and to the point; I expect my team to understand my frequency.
- I am usually busy and do not have time for coaching the team; I expect them to know what I need.

Now discover and evaluate each roadblock. Think of it as a real drone and see how it is doing. Be honest and review how well you are flying it.

- ☐ **Fully autonomous flight**
- ☐ **Guided flights**
- ☐ **Irregular flight path**
- ☐ **Unwilling to take off**

#KeyResonatingActions

- Learn about your (information) consumer(s)—their background, understanding, expectations and assumptions. Most of them will be happy to provide this information and would appreciate the additional effort.
- Provide as much context, mitigation and potential actions while communicating difficult or unpleasant information.
- Avoid broadcasting as much as possible and send contextual updates to different categories of stakeholders based on their need.
- Seek constant feedback, especially what the stakeholders like about your communication.
- Plan ahead. Right timing of sharing information is as important as sharing the information itself.
- Be mindful of frequency and relevance of information shared. People tend to eventually ignore communication:
    - o From individuals whose information doesn't provoke action or invoke thought process.
    - o If information is sent too many times without giving sufficient time in between.

AS A LEADER, ONE MUST

- Set up forums where the protocols of communication and effectiveness of communication in the team are discussed frequently.
- Ask the team to come up with avenues where there is 'information waste', that is, information is sent which no one is consuming.
- Appreciate and exemplify good communication by individuals.
- Frequently review the communication protocols—internal as well as external.
- Coach the team on pre and post activities of information sharing, which will help the stakeholders better appreciate the information shared and take necessary actions.
- Be an empathetic bridge of the team for organizational communication—to explain the relevance, action required and results of inaction.
- Where possible, have a role of communication champion to constantly measure and improve the practices of information sharing in the team.

#StickyNoteWorthy

The art of communication is the language of leadership.

James Humes

Communication which is clean, empathetic and personalized takes a lot of thought and effort to prepare and deliver. But it is worth the effort! It is an unfailing means of success employed by successful individuals and effective leaders. They also bring forth a reassuring body language, confidence in articulation, honesty in messaging and clear 'not hazardous, all okay, don't worry!' signs with them when they speak.

2

MOP STICK

On Ownership and Accountability

'Sparkling clean now! If we are happy, then the guests will also be happy, right sir?' Ramu remarked at the service supervisor as he came out of the deluxe room of Taj hotel in Mumbai, where he worked as a room service and cleaning boy. The supervisor gave a nod and went through the checklist of items which needed to be replaced for the guest arriving that day. 'I will take one final look, sir,' said Ramu and quickly checked the room and the toilet. 'Feels fresh, now we can go,' he wiped his name badge pinned to his shirt and straightened his shirt. 'You do that every time we come out of the room, Ramu?' asked his supervisor. 'Yes, sir, I am proud of it; this job makes me stand on my own two feet and my parents proud. I still don't believe I am not at the port catching fish…,' he smiled.

Ramu was recruited by Taj Hotels a year ago. He hailed from a poor fisherman's family of Ratnagiri, a port town in Maharashtra, and was destined to follow his family tradition. Getting the opportunity to join Taj has been 'a life changing event…', he would tell his fellow mates and supervisors at least once every day. 'That boy has a smile plastered permanently on his face. Never seen him worn out of it,' remarked one of his supervisors to their superintendent after their morning huddle. 'I see him recite the company values at the start of each day,' he added.

The staff worked like clockwork day and night, receiving guests cheerfully and maintaining an aura of happiness and joy. It was one such day when Mr Swaminathan arrived at Taj. As a vice president at a global corporation, he was visiting Mumbai briefly for few days over business matters and checked in on a hot and humid afternoon. 'Your room is ready, sir; you will be escorted by Mahesh here, and we will bring your luggage to the room shortly,' said the receptionist softly as she welcomed Mr Swaminathan. He gave the impression of being a hard-to-please middle-aged strict disciplinarian, who was not happy to be away from home and demanded a natural order and respect from all those around him. The receptionist called for Ramu. Ramu noticed the slightly worn-out but sturdy walking stick on which Mr Swaminathan was leaning on as he took each step, and seemingly in slight discomfort with his right leg. He was escorted dutifully to his room and as Ramu gently placed his suitcase in the holder beside the door, he wished a pleasant, 'Taj wishes you a pleasant stay, sir, we are here for you,' and left the room.

Ramu visited Mr Swaminathan's room for room service the next couple of days. He noticed that Mr Swaminathan was a man of few words—crisp and direct. He kept an extremely strict routine; he arrived at breakfast exactly at 8 AM each day and had just buttermilk at dinner. Ramu promptly wished him each time there was an encounter, and all Mr Swaminathan would do was give a curt nod at the boy. One day, Mr Swaminathan briefly paused and noticed the mop stick in Ramu's hands as he was cleaning away what seemed to be a stain in the hallway. 'It is nothing, sir, shall I bring up your buttermilk in 30 minutes?' Ramu asked with a smile. And there was that nod again.

The next day, Ramu noticed that Mr Swaminathan returned earlier than usual and was assisted by another young man wearing a tie. 'Something seems amiss!' Ramu thought to himself and continued with his work. At sharp 7.30 PM, Ramu softly knocked at the door, 'Sir, room service. I have brought your buttermilk.' 'Come in,' came a tired reply. Ramu gently opened the door and walked in like a soldier approaching the general to receive a medal with a tray in his hands. As he placed the tray on the table beside the sofa, he heard angry mumbling from Mr Swaminathan which was unusual for him, 'How on earth can I misplace it! Serves me right to get bureaucratic and walk around without my stick as if I have no limp. What was wrong with being myself…?'

'Can I please help you with something, sir?' Ramu spoke with utmost concern.

'Can you walk me to the bathroom, what's it, Ramu?' Mr Swaminathan strained his eyes to read the name tag on Ramu's shirt. 'Certainly, sir!'

Then it hit Ramu. He recollected that the young boy with the tie was escorting Mr Swaminathan to his room earlier in the day. His walking stick was missing! He must have misplaced it. 'Oh! how difficult it must be for him without his stick. He is supposed to leave tomorrow afternoon, and he will not have time for getting another one, and looks like he is not around from Mumbai,' Ramu wiped his badge involuntarily lost in deep thought. Then it hit him, and he smiled broadly, 'At Taj, no one stays unhappy,' and he made a dash for it.

Next morning at 7.50 AM, Ramu went up to the room of Mr Swaminathan and knocked softly, 'Sir, room service.'

'What is it? I didn't call for you, what do you want?' came a stern reply.

'Please, sir, may I enter?' persisted Ramu.

Mr Swaminathan walked to the door with discomfort and let Ramu in.

'Sir, please take this, compliments from Taj for you,' and handed over what looked like his lost stick, but it was not the same!

'What! Where?! What is this Ramu…,' Mr Swaminathan stammered in shock and Ramu could see that he was clearly overjoyed.

'Wait a minute, now I see it,' Mr Swaminathan noticed the small inscription of Taj Hotels on the stick towards the bottom. 'Bless you dear boy! This is a mopping stick. How on earth did you do this Ramu?' he took Ramu's hand in his affectionately as he leaned on his new makeshift walking stick with his other hand.

'Sir, at Taj it is our utmost responsibility that all our guests are happy and satisfied. When I saw you in discomfort yesterday, I did not know what else to do. I did not want to disturb my manager or anyone else. I took my mopping stick to Gokhale uncle, who is a carpenter, and requested him to change it like this. I am happy to see that you like it,' Ramu smiled ear to ear.

'Like it? My dear boy, you have made your company proud. No, you have put Taj on the map. This behaviour is inconceivable. Who teaches you these things? This is the most touching compliment I have ever received. Are you telling me you did all this without even informing your manager?' Mr Swaminathan spoke fast and did not believe what he just heard from Ramu. How could a room service boy take on such a responsibility on his own and act out of humanity and genuine concern, without expecting any favour! Such commitment was unheard of in his long career so far.

'Why, sir? At Taj we take our responsibilities very seriously. It is my job to keep you happy. I did not need to ask anyone. I am sure my management would be supportive,' Ramu spoke sincerely. 'I will make sure they are much more than supportive, dear boy. Will you please take me to your manager?' Mr Swaminathan put his hand kindly on Ramu's shoulder. 'Surely, sir,' said Ramu, and as he stepped out, he gently wiped his badge and smiled.

Ramu now serves as the general manager of one of the prestigious Taj Hotels in the country, and Ramu's heroics are one of several tales of pride and customer centricity that Taj and Tata have displayed for generations.*

#WorkplaceWhispers

Taking complete ownership of one's job and being accountable with pride are undoubtedly seen as two excellent attributes of an individual in any organization. Such individuals tend to gain visibility and get entrusted with more opportunities (usually regardless of successes or failures). These two attributes are cornerstones and steppingstones to leadership positions. However, these are perhaps the most difficult to master.

As we have seen from this real-life incident, Mr Swaminathan was not one of the pleasant customers which Ramu interacted with. And he could have simply ignored Swaminathan's pain. However, he chose to display true dedication and sensitivity in discovering that something was wrong with his customer and chose to act. And even when he did that, he could have gone straight to his manager and asked for help. But his sense of ownership and accountability in keeping his customer happy did not let him take any chance, nor delegate the problem to someone else.

Taj management also displayed values of 'respecting the individual' and appreciating Ramu's display of customer centricity, instead of reprimanding him for wasting the mop stick of the company or missing the opportunity to charge the customer in buying a new walking stick. Instead, they chose to make this an exemplary tale, a heroic story which every associate of the hotel should listen to, and further bolstered the value

* Narrative based on true incidents, with names changed for anonymity.

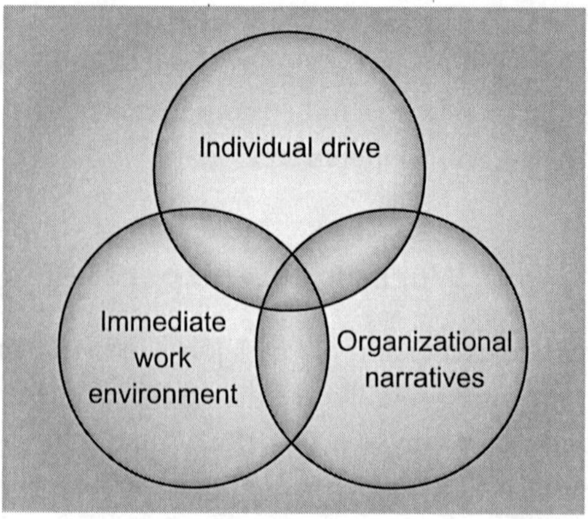

Figure 2.1 Ownership and Accountability

system and principles of Ramu, enabling him to succeed further in his career.

Perhaps the biggest dilemma which associates tend to entertain while approaching the attributes of ownership and accountability is whether they are related to one's role and position (of authority) in the organization! The answer to this dilemma lies across three dimensions (as shown in Figure 2.1).

1. *Individual drive:* One's attitude, belief system and ability to apply oneself.
2. *Organizational narratives:* What is heard/discussed in the company constantly.
3. *Immediate work environment:* Your current work environment.

When all three factors are congenial, there is no doubt that at an individual level these attributes have a greater possibility to shine and thrive.

However, those who power ahead of the others in their career are the ones who rely more on the first dimension and tend to contribute to the other two positively. And they do it with a sense of belonging (accountability) and love (ownership) for the job.

Let me quote a few examples from my experience.

'JUST ABOUT TO LEAVE'

One is that of Mr Keshav Varma, a senior business leader and one of my mentors. This incident happened several double-digit years ago, when Keshav was a junior support engineer working with a North American customer. It was a late Friday evening. Keshav was wrapping up his shift, working on the handover formalities to the night shift associate coming in shortly and was just about to leave. Then came a ping from an ailing customer who was having trouble with one of the applications not working well. The easy thing to do would have been to silently minimize the window, lock the computer and move on as if nothing happened. Keshav chose to work on the issue. He not only sat through another couple of hours to address the problem but also provided useful tips to the customer so that the issue could be prevented from occurring again. The customer happened to be a senior executive, who ensured that the junior support engineer was duly recognized.

#How do you reward such motivated associates in your team?

'LEARNING CANNOT BE DELEGATED'

The other experience also dates back several years ago when I was working with one Mr M. C. M. Raju, who was the leader of our group responsible for quality assurance (QA) for the entire unit. We used to see him regularly carry bulky volumes of ITIL and other such frameworks and prepare extensive documents. He would invite us to discuss specific aspects and draw a correlation between theory and project context. When we questioned him on why he was taking the pain despite being in such a senior role and employing experts from the team to do the job, he used to smile and say, 'How do I know that they are doing a good job? If my understanding is good, then it is easy to elevate and appreciate the work done by my team.'

I am sure you have seen such exemplary individuals yourself (including one every day in the mirror), who live the principles of ownership and accountability by their sheer drive and passion and also contribute positively to the organizational narratives as well as nurture the work environment.

'ONE THING FOR THE GROWTH OF...'

Another powerful way to understand ownership and accountability is to think of the difference we could make to each other's lives. Here is a powerful advice from Amit Bajaj, Corporate Vice President—Markets at TCS, to a group of young managers during one of his interactions, 'All of you are good in your own areas and understand the needs of your customers well, I am sure of that. Here's one more thing you should do constantly—think about one thing that will help your customer grow and put your efforts to make it happen. You will gain a lot in return—respect, relationship and tremendous learning.'

#GameofDrones

- I do not understand the positive impact which I can bring in with my work.
- I am not aware of or fully appreciate the intent behind my company values and my personal value system; I rarely rely on it when faced with tough challenges at work.
- I have a vague understanding of who my customers are and how my work impacts them.

- I am so busy with work that I do not spend time regularly to explore the big opportunity I have based on my current work context and position.
- I usually keep silent during team interactions and do not share the positive influences of my work with my colleagues and contribute to the organizational narratives.
- (As a manager) I rarely speak about company values and encourage the team to derive practical implications of the same at workplace.
- I hesitate to give control to my team in their own boundary and tend to feel insecure by their actions (especially when they do something without my knowledge).

Now discover and evaluate each roadblock. Think of it as a real drone and see how it is doing. Be honest and review how well you are flying it.

- ☐ **Fully autonomous flight**
- ☐ **Guided flights**
- ☐ **Irregular flight path**
- ☐ **Unwilling to take off**

#KeyResonatingActions

AS AN INDIVIDUAL

- Be persistent and regular in seeking feedback.
- Try to understand the big picture—a useful exercise is to rename one's title to reflect the impact on customer or outcomes delivered; for example, instead of calling oneself a business analyst, try 'specialist in uncovering automation potential'.

- Share and celebrate experiences of customer (or colleague) delight with the others in the team; this helps charge the work environment.
- Take a medium- to long-term view of the current opportunity; seek help from a mentor in putting this together.
- Smile often; you would be amazed at how many would contribute to your learning cheerfully if you just lower the guard and be more approachable.

AS A LEADER

- Encourage forums where the big picture of the work is discussed, and how the work done by the team impacts the customer. I have seen that most associates spend years in a team without understanding the big picture.
- Make appreciation a part of day-to-day work experience. Appreciate those who displayed accountability and ownership at their level.
- Be a champion of your company values and the founding principles of your organization.

#StickyNoteWorthy

Just don't give up trying to do what you really want to do. Where there is love and inspiration, I don't think you can go wrong.

Ella Fitzgerald

In any organization, the needle is moved forward by resolute individuals who are not afraid to stand up, ask questions, walk the extra mile and leverage every opportunity to dive in and resurface. And those organizations which take care of such individuals stand apart and thrive.

3 ON THE SIDELINES

Dealing with Naysayers

2035 AD: VIJAYAWADA

'Rohit, your shave efficiency is 75 per cent compared to all men of your age who shaved this morning,' came a digital voice from the smart shaver. 'Yeah? Where did I miss the rest 25 per cent?' Rohit asked with a raised eyebrow.

'Contacting Shaverzine … downloading … ready! The answer to your question with detailed follicle and shave pattern analysis will take approximately 3.5 minutes for me to update, but your schedule tells me that you are already late for your next event; the bath shower is sending alerts; do you want me to still run you through the analysis?' asked the shaver.

'Oh no! Save it for later; I would want to be in the high 90s,' Rohit ran to take the shower.

'Would like to take the 2-minute shower programme today,' he yelled.

'Initiating…,' came a digital response, as water jutted through the pores along with a fine mix of organic body wash. As he took the shower, he shouted another command, 'Send remark hash shaver 9910 hash—need crisper shave analysis—end remark.' A device that looked like a green bug on the wall responded with a soft ding and 'Remark sent'.

'Refill shampoo supplies in two days, place automatic order…,' Rohit did not wait for the shower to finish the update.

Today was his big day. He would be facing the infamous 'sideline squad' at Phuntronics Ltd. Rohit Sarna worked in applied anthropomorphism (AA) department at the company and had joined the firm recently after completing his PhD from Takshasila University, which is supposed to be the best in the world for advanced sustainable and safe robotics (ASSR).

The university was proud of producing many scientists who played a key role in the advancement of and shaping the world thinking in the right usage of the art of robotics and applied sensible intelligence, but two programmes of the university particularly stood apart in which no other university of the world came even closer—robotic psychology and robotic anthropomorphism. Rohit specialized from Takshasila and was picked up by Phuntronics Ltd as one of the fast-track candidates.

'Proximity full biometric scan complete ... authorizing Rohit to Phuntronics Ltd Robotic Division,' came the voice and the doors slid open as he walked closer to the entry barrier. 'No matter what, these digital voices would never sound human to me,' he thought as he entered the premises.

'Hey there, Sheila!' he waved at a colleague who joined him along in the hallway which led up to the presentation area. A 3-feet house-elf type robot with a sadistic expression on his face whizzed past them both and hurled an insult, 'Are you prepared to face the fun, loser?'

'Keep your calm,' said Sheila before Rohit could react. 'I am sure J. K. Rowling would be proud of these creatures now,' he said. 'That is mean; not all her house elves were mean!' replied Sheila, 'The sideline squad is designed to be mean; he is doing his job.'

'How do you know it's a "he"?' laughed Rohit to hide his anxiety as he tried to set his tie straight.

'Phuntronics Ltd was set up by one of the brightest dropouts from Takshasila, Santha Ramani. Although she did not complete her education there, she incorporated all the robotic ethics professed by the university. "The sideline squad" was one of the genius ideas in action from Santha,' Rohit recollected the debrief from his mentor as he walked to the room in silence. 'These robots are always on the "sidelines"; they never contribute to real work, and their sole purpose is to sneer, but share continuous feedback,' she said.

'But Laks, why have they been designed to be so brutal? Couldn't the feedback be much kinder?' Rohit retorted.

'Well, if you clear the sideline squad, then your model will go through any levels of stringent scrutiny by any authority in the world; they have access to the world database of feedback collected by zillions of connected devices placed all over the world. The "remarks" are streamed in real time and fed into the squad instantly. Of course, the devices listen to only those people who have consented to share information, so we are compliant to Robotic Data Privacy Regulations, and we don't listen to anything else,' said Laks, 'We also display the top 100 funniest remarks on robots made by people, in our dashboard.'

'This is insane, but I guess important to know the psychological aspects of human interactions with robots,' Rohit sighed.

'Not just that, the sideline squad also has a handle on the alpha-level research of Takshasila, which no other company apart from Phuntronics Ltd has access to. That is priceless! That makes them the best squad to evaluate any new model. Don't worry, you are one of our brightest, you will do well. A 50 per cent pass is all you need to clear; the highest we have seen so far is 65per cent and that robot is still in business, most loved by our customers,' said Laks.

'There is another reason behind creating this squad and that name. Our founder Santha believed that two types of associates ruin the company—those who do not take concrete actions but only complain sitting on the sidelines and those who cannot tolerate feedback. The sideline squad is a reminder of these two principles and to robotically nudge everyone not to get into that trap. You will face an extreme level of humiliation starting tomorrow until you are cleared, even if you have to make a 50 per cent score,' she smiled.

Rohit gently turned the handle down and opened the door. There was a slight buzz as the 20 mean-looking robots sitting in a semicircular formation around a huge table exchanged words.

'What melodrama! They are just robots; they are mimicking human behaviours, that too one of the most despicable ones; you can face this; you are tough!' Rohit told himself.

He heard laughter from the robots which appeared like 'ducks speaking to each other in Morse code'—'Eh eh eh, are you the new recruit? Don't you think you need to spend more time with Phuntronics before facing the squad?' said a robot sitting on one side of the table. 'Don't bother answering that; Where's your toy? Invoke the model,' said another.

Rohit walked to the centre of the room and tapped on his wrist. Two tiles on the floor in front of him slid aside. A beautiful humanoid robot emerged and opened her eyes.

'Do you have a stupid name? Eh, aren't you a girl?' asked someone.

'Yes, I can shape shift at the initial configuration time as per user preferences; settings include change of gender, height, age, nationality and cultural background, and you can give me a name, might I suggest a few options?' came a kind reply.

'Nope! Initiate compliance scans. Expose your access points; for this evaluation, we will call you Eva,' came another command. The girl nodded and lifted both her arms, and an intricate web of digital interfaces shot up around her, almost clouding her form. All the 20 robots scanned through the connectors, making noises in between. 'Compliance scans barely passed, we expected better performance than this, initiating security scans…'

That was a good sign for Rohit. Moving to next stage meant that his robot is making progress with the squad. After the fundamental checks were done, the squad moved on to evaluating the model with their anthropomorphic feedback.

'Hair is unrealistic, rough texture, waterproof?' asked a robot. 'Adjustable and waterproof', answered Eva.

'Last time an angry customer remarked that his robot had a stupid smile even when someone passed away in the family; can your face show an empathetic expression?' Eva mimicked a sad face and said, 'I feel sorry to be around you all.' 'Not yet, we will get there soon,' jeered another robot.

The evaluation continued for many hours where Eva was scrutinized for her ability to react and respond to several human interactions and circumstances. After this, the squad said, 'We will observe the robot in action for the next few days, in simulated contexts. You score a 49 per cent for today's performance, but this is not the final mark; we are sure you would score much lower overall once we are through with this,' and they all laughed again in unison.

'Who designed these maniacs?' Rohit could not control his anger as he met Sheila and Laks outside the presentation room. 'A 49 per cent is a good score, if the squad agreed to the next stage,' said Laks. 'Technically, you are through if you get couple of more percentage points from your colleagues, after further manual evaluation,' said Sheila.

'No, I want to go through the next round with the squad and do the full review. Would like to see what they bring forth,' replied Rohit.

In the next few days, as Rohit worked with Eva, the sideline squad would pop in and comment on anything ranging from the looks of Eva to the working style of Rohit. 'You are not working enough with your prog bots. Have you checked what runtime they are on?... Have you fixed compliance issues yet? Do you know that when you fix an observation, your robot should initiate a review uplink to the sideline squad?… Your working hours can be better; ensure consistency for better productivity….'

'Can you guys ever shut up and not get personal with my work style,' yelled Rohit once. 'Stop commenting and do something for a change'. 'Eh … eh … eh … eh … eh,' they laughed and left his zone. 'I will quit this company if Santha doesn't authorize someone to at least fix this annoying dumb digital laughter,' he kicked the door shut.

The sideline squad continued with their visits. As he got used to this, Rohit realized that there is an element of improvement in every remark they threw at him. Afterall, these robots are designed to synthesize and relay 'what can improve', although in an insulting manner. It made him more resolute and although he did not accept every insult thrown at him, very soon he learnt to handle the sideline squad with ease and comfort. Even more, he started to have fun with these interactions and waited for their surprise visits.

'It appeared to me initially that no one insulted me so much, but as I looked closely, they are not making aimless remarks. I am paying attention to every comment made as it is based on either a real-world feedback or a regulatory norm; Eva is getting better and better,' he told Laks with enthusiasm.

This change in his attitude also meant that he worked with improved focus and enthusiasm on Eva. 'I like the name; maybe there is a reason they just threw that name at you,' he once told his robot. 'It's short and two syllables; most people would find it easy to utter, even those with mild speaking disabilities…,' replied the robot, 'But, hey, its configurable.'

'Welcome, guys,' he said when the two robots from the squad came in next day. 'Eh … eh … eh … eh,' they turned around and left.

'Strange!' said Eva. 'I heard you remark last week that you are looking forward to their visit, and yesterday when they visited our zone while you were away, I welcomed them, and they immediately left making that annoying laughter!' exclaimed Eva mimicking an expression of surprise on her face.

'Drop theatrics,' Rohit issued a command and Eva retracted her face to normal.

'I have a changed opinion on their laughter too Eva,' he smiled, and she mimicked his smile.

'A final score of 64.5 per cent, our CEO wants to meet you Rohit; this is close to being historical, although I wanted you to cross 65,' Laks conveyed the results to Rohit. 'The blueprint will now be sent for final approval before authorizing a pilot production for select geographies and globally scaled later,' she added.

'I should've scored 0.5 per cent more indeed,' Rohit raised his shoulders, 'But if it's good enough for a meet with CEO, I'd settle for that.'

'The sideline squad was designed with the purpose of inflicting tough feedback to our designers, especially in your area of anthropomorphism...,' Santha spoke calmly, 'Most design teams aim to cross the 50 per cent mark and ship the robot to the next phase. They find it hard to tolerate the scrutiny with these robots. Very few attempt to take on the challenge all the way through. Apart from the synthesized input from the outside world, the sideline squad is also fed with inputs on the failure models, the ones which never hit the production line and that is 80 per cent of the models which have hit the 50 per cent pass mark! But not many care about that; their KPI is crossing this scrutiny alone.'

Rohit listened intently with deep respect. Getting an audience with the CEO in the first year at Phuntronics was not even close to being his dream.

'You did well, Rohit. I would like more of our employees to go through the realization that you've experienced and learn to evaluate inputs keenly beyond the periphery,' she said.

'At least we don't have anyone sitting on the sidelines and only making comments, Santha, thanks to the squad; no one likes to mimic this behaviour. All our employees believe in execution and that's an important thing we've achieved,' replied Rohit.

'Yes! Only the sideline squad can sit on the sidelines and complain about everything and everyone at Phuntronics. By the way, your rash behaviour once with the squad when you yelled at them, there went your 0.5 per cent. I was the one that scored 65 per cent after we launched the squad,' Santha winked.

'What about the rest 35 per cent?' Rohit enquired.

'They are observations and inputs for the subsequent phases of production preparation based on your model, past data and a lot of proprietary AI; it is technically not a feedback for this stage. It is a reminder to state that your work is only 65 per cent done, and the robot will see its life, provided the rest of the observations are met too,' she smiled.

'That is an awesome way to score and inculcate end-to-end thinking! Thank you for your time and appreciation,' remarked Rohit as he took her leave.

'Closing the meeting, Phuntronics Ltd wishes you a very good evening,' came the digital voice as Rohit removed his advanced extended reality (AXR) headset after the CEO meet and stepped out of his working room at his home. He put on his smart shoes and prepared to go for a jog.

'Initiating jog counters, weight 72 Kg....'

'Switch off,' Rohit issued a break command and took off with a smile on his face.

#WorkplaceWhispers

Organizations are constantly subject to the forces of market demands, expectations (internal and external), regulations, security, operational efficiency and so on. This would mean that the workforce and the workplace have also been continuously evolving and expanding (either in size or complexity). Regardless of the size of the company which you may be working at, I am sure you must be constantly interacting with multiple groups interfacing with you/your team and delivering to diverse needs of your company. And chances are that all of those groups do not always have priorities aligned, leading to what most of us experience (sooner or later) as 'process drag'—in the form of someone (or a workflow) saying, 'Nay! You have to slow down champ.'

'THEY KEEP GETTING IN THE WAY'

'Okay, from today there is this new process; you must take all your proposals through this unit for approval and by the way they are very busy, so plan ahead and don't run to them in the last minute.' For someone like you and me, that is not a pretty line to read. It feels like 'Don't these guys have anything else to do than get in between me and the wonderful stuff I would like to deliver?'

But this is a reality, sometimes pushed by external forces (regulations) and sometimes by organizational drive to be more efficient. Also, quality and security are sacrosanct, and it is wise to embrace directives in these areas while trying to simplify their implementation with continuous feedback.

'BUT WE CAN BE FASTER, LIKE THE START-UPS...'

So much is spoken about the start-up culture and how large organizations should continuously try to remain start-ups in their heart. Easier said than done! And unless forged from the ground up by leaders with a digital native mentality, chances are that the start-ups eventually might grow large and shake hands with the same problems as any other large organization would.

However, one element of the start-up culture which any organization/team can borrow is *belongingness to the goal/vision of the start-up*—that's what keeps everybody together. Each group 'knows' that the other group (no matter what restrictions they seem to put) believes in the end goal as much as they do. *Empathy* is a common denominator there, and this enables every associate in a start-up not to *give up* on each other, feel empowered and drive the change which they wish to see. These elements can be adopted by any team to help them work with a positive attitude and not give up on each other. There are countless times when I did exactly the opposite, that is, throw up hands in the air saying, 'This is hopeless; these guys have no clue what pain we go through; all they want to show us is how important they are,' before I calmed down and focused on what can be done better than being dramatic.

POWER OF NO

There are two derailers at an individual level which tend to get exhibited when faced with a 'No!' First one is to complain and give up too soon—I have seen associates talking about quitting a project team because they get stuck with the peripheral 'No' and don't make the attempt to dig deeper. 'That person doesn't like me and hence he rejects my work. I worked extremely hard to do this. I want to move out of this team,' they would say. And second one is to complain silently but follow along just to get over the hump one way or the other.

Being in the position of saying 'No' comes with a great responsibility—to uplift the quality of work or safeguard the organization/team—but it need not be exercised in a hurtful manner.

And learning to survive the 'No' and go beyond it is a hallmark of successful individuals.

REAL NAYSAYER

'Is us…,' says Shrivathsa A., a young business development manager. 'We cannot give up on ourselves and get stuck with "it is not possible." There were instances when I had to persist for over eight months before convincing others on the merit of the idea and find a way forward. Once we believe in something genuinely, we got to keep trying, in multiple ways, and not fall trap to self-doubt,' he adds.

#GameofDrones

AS AN INDIVIDUAL

- I do not appreciate nor try to understand the so-called compliance checks in my company; they are bottlenecks to productivity.
- The support groups often introduce delays; they ask for so much proof, sometimes it is as if they don't know what they want.
- I don't try to understand the priorities of these (naysaying) groups and vice versa.
- In general, I do not want to interact with people sitting on the sidelines and not contributing; they are a burden to the company.
- I have found some loopholes in the process and know exactly what it takes to clear the checks.
- I find it easy to manage the support groups by complaining loudly; there is not enough time to plan, and escalation works better.

BEING IN THE ROLE OF SAYING NO

- I take my job very seriously and reject everything that doesn't meet my requirements; sometimes I reject on the fly and don't have the time to explain why.
- This is a lonely job; no one likes to talk to me, and I return the favour all the time.
- This has been the process for as long as I remember; we don't see the need to simplify it or change it.

AS A LEADER

- I let the team deal with the naysaying groups; I have better things to focus on.
- I do not want to be in the bad books of anyone by giving feedback; first the teams complain but eventually they settle down.

Now discover and evaluate each roadblock. Think of it as a real drone and see how it is doing. Be honest and review how well you are flying it.

- ☐ **Fully autonomous flight**
- ☐ **Guided flights**
- ☐ **Irregular flight path**
- ☐ **Unwilling to take off**

#KeyResonatingActions

AS AN INDIVIDUAL

- As much as possible, plan ahead and try to understand the potential checks in the project end to end.

- When faced with a rejection, request for clarifications and interact with empathy—this could be an opportunity to lift your work further.
- Always be open to share additional information and make the experience of working with you easy; this will go a long way and subsequent interactions will be much smoother.
- If you see a process gap, share feedback via the right channel (or directly as appropriate).
- Make the naysayers (process guardians) part of your story—provide context of what you do and how this will benefit the organization.
- Be empathetic to those who seem to be sitting on the sidelines and not contributing—avoid being judgemental and try to learn their perspective.

BEING THE NAYSAYER

- Constantly revisit your processes to check their relevance and simplify without compromising efficiency.
- Solicit levers of digital and automation to bring in more agility.
- Conduct roadshows or awareness sessions to the interfacing teams.
- Provide guidance on how the quality of work can be improved.
- Be empathetic in language and kind in communication.

AS A LEADER

- Encourage the team to proactively find 'waste' in the project activities and how this knowledge can be applied creatively in the upcoming projects.

- Organize meet-ups between the delivery teams and process teams to discuss the upcoming milestones and pre-empt bottlenecks.
- Encourage constant feedback from the team and work with them to prepare action plans.
- Be sensitive to the contributions made by the associates in the team, and if there is any process slack that is making anyone sit on the sidelines and wait.
- Be the champion of sharing your team's feedback to the larger organization; this is a great way to drive change and bond with the team.

#StickyNoteWorthy

One of the truest tests of integrity is its blunt refusal to be compromised.

Chinua Achebe

Being *purpose-driven* and walking *until the last mile is conquered* are attributes to develop and also encourage in others. This would mean not only embracing hurdles in the stride but also working on long-term solutions hand in hand with the others. As teams and organizations work with empathy and mutual respect, without losing sight of the end goal, naysayers/naysaying will be embraced as a key step in the larger game.

4

FINDING YOUR LEVEL

A long time ago, near the banks of river Godavari and cuddled between the beautiful Papi Hills was a small village by name Kummaripalle (village of the potters). The village people were very friendly with each other, and with the natural resources they had, they were largely self-sufficient. One of the main professions of the village was making earthenware and sculptures out of clay. There was a community of clay sculptors and potters which used to make beautiful pieces of pottery, idols and other earthenware and sell it to the nearby villages and towns. The earthenware and the crafts made of this village were incredibly famous.

Given that the village was close to the riverbank and the surrounding hilly region, there was an abundance of all types of clay for the potters and sculptors. The quality of the clay (from where it was dug out and how well it was prepared) of course determined the quality of the craft made of it. However, the process involved in getting the clay out of the riverbanks and other areas and cleansing it to the right level was a long and difficult one.

Hailing from a family of potters who had been making pottery and sculptures out of clay for generations, Gopal could not learn the art no matter how hard he tried. Even Gopal's brothers turned out to be decent craftsmen and made a good living. Gopal's father tried hard to inspire the lad and somehow ignite the spark of the ancestral skill. But much to his dismay and that of the community, Gopal remained an incorrigible exception. It did not take long for the community to give up on him.

However, he was not willing to let himself down and continued with his efforts. He started experimenting with different types of clay which he secured from riverbeds at multiple locations and streambeds of streams running through the hills. 'Maybe there is another texture of clay which will work for my hands,' he thought and continued to explore places where no potter ever went before. But his hands simply lacked the dexterity needed to mould the clay. He started visiting elders of the community to see them work and tried to understand several aspects of making pottery more keenly. Unknowingly, he also mentally noted the difficulties involved in making a good product. 'If only my hands got to a mound of mud with a better consistency, I could make marvels out of it,' he often heard the seniors of the community remark.

'See, Gopal, my work starts only after the clay comes to a refined state without all these impurities and then I can focus on making a fine piece of art,' said his neighbour when Gopal was watching him prepare the clay. 'Why are you wasting your time with that boy!' Gopal heard his father pass by and shouting at the neighbour.

As usual, the next day Gopal went farther upstream than ever before in his small boat. His eyes spotted what seemed like a thick sticky deposit on the riverbank. He checked the consistency of the clay and screamed 'clay from heaven!' He moved further along the bank and to his great delight there was a reserve of the same material in huge deposits. 'I am sure I can make good pottery out of this, finally!' he thought. 'I was looking for you all my life; I will name you after me, the Gopal clay!' he laughed at himself for the silly thought. As he started gathering the clay into the sack which he carried with him, he thought of all the interactions he had with the village potters and sculptors. Then it struck him, 'I should stop running around for myself and finding clay which will fit me. What if I cannot wield the craft myself, I will help others make better products!'

Gopal realized that if only he could solve the problems of the community in preparing the clay to the right level, they could focus their time on making better products. He suddenly felt a new purpose in life—'I will be the first clay supplier of the village!' he announced to himself.

From the very next day, Gopal started gathering heaps of clay from different spots he uncovered and refining it into multiple levels of consistency. He met with different craftsmen to understand their needs and started to supply them the needed clay material. This made the village craftsmen extremely happy and with someone helping them with their fundamental problem to such a refined degree, they started producing the best earthenware and clay sculptures in the entire kingdom, so much so that the fame of Kummaripalle reached their king in due time. 'These sculptures are as hard as iron and as smooth as marble,' remarked one of the ministers to the king. 'My wife makes delicious meals out of these earthenware, O king! This is truly remarkable craftsmanship!'

The king himself came down to visit the village to understand the secret, and as he rewarded the top craftsmen of the village including Gopal's father, they all humbly pointed to the king the contributions of Gopal. 'Here, O king, is the person who lifted our level!' they said in unison.

'My dear fellow, I am very happy to note your contributions to the craft. How did you develop this skill?' asked the king to the utter joy of the entire village including the parents of Gopal.

'Your majesty! Although I was born in a family of potters, my father too being an excellent craftsman whom you have so worthily rewarded just now, I had the great misfortune of not carrying my ancestral skill. Although everyone around me gave up, I proceeded with sheer determination to explore on my own. Every taunt pushed me to keenly learn the end-to-end process and uncover that one piece of clay that my hands can mould. But one day, the clay indeed taught me the real secret. It moulded my thought processes—I shifted the focus from my disability to how I can help those around me with the unique knowledge I have developed.

Maybe the lack of skill in my hands was for a reason; it helped everyone else around me become more skilful with their craft,' concluded Gopal in a humble tone.

'And for that, my dear fellow, you will be rewarded the most!' praised the king rewarding Gopal with a lot of gifts and compliments.

#WorkplaceWhispers

'AM I HEADED IN THE RIGHT DIRECTION?'

When you are new to the team and still getting acquainted with the processes and workflows, you look for a flicker of approval or a connect with a teammate to appease your nervous and unsure guts and tell you that you are doing okay. When the initial years are through and you suddenly find yourself to be in the thick of things, your circle of the 'team' also expands, and the uncertainty and anxiety-filled question marks come back. 'Am I or my team valuable enough for our customers? Does my team appreciate my initiatives and the interactions I have with them? Am I considered part of their circle of "team" or are they responding to me just out of formality or fear?'

In my first onshore assignment as a manager several years ago, I came across a senior director in the customer organization who would go to extreme lengths to check how her initiatives were being received by her unit. She would remark in our lunch conversations, 'For one, being assertive and taking charge is important, but even more important is not to lose your team, Phani!' Here, I thought it was just me!

It is true that everyone in the workplace, even the seniormost of associates, constantly battles with such dilemmas. But the truth which escapes some of us is that these dilemmas are not borne out of lack of confidence on one's skills or authority. On the contrary, they arise because one cares deeply and wishes to contribute by staying relevant.

As I grew up in my career from being a trainee out of college to heading a large team overseas, finding answers to the changing flavours of these dilemmas helped me take more initiatives, be proactive, get involved and seek constant feedback.

#GameofDrones

- I constantly compare myself with others in the team and get self-critical or uncomfortable with my skill level.
- (If the answer to the above is yes) I do not take the initiative to ask for help and get coached to improve upon my deficiencies.
- I am unaware of what complementary (non-core) skills I possess which can be leveraged in the team.
- I do not understand the big picture view of the work being done in the team.
- I do not enquire proactively the challenges faced by my colleague(s) and help them with improving their quality of work.
- As a manager, I tend to be in a hurry and not take the time to explain 'why' I am asking 'what' I am asking, and define the right level of the output expected.

- My team never asks questions upfront, but I find that what they deliver is seldom up to the mark, leading to frustration and multiple iterations.
- I tend to show preferential appreciation to only certain individuals or skills in the team, as they are most value adding to my unit.
- I am not aware of any artists or individuals with exceptional skills in my team, as I do not think that such non-core skills are relevant for us.

Now discover and evaluate each roadblock. Think of it as a real drone and see how it is doing. Be honest and review how well you are flying it.

☐ **Fully autonomous flight**

☐ **Guided flights**

☐ **Irregular flight path**

☐ **Unwilling to take off**

#KeyResonatingActions

- Try to find areas where you could offer help to another (senior/expert) individual of the team.
- Constantly ask for the big picture and both the context and constraints involved in the work—this will help you find areas where you could contribute further.
- Seek feedback often and be approachable.
- Share feedback; most times people do not understand what you are going through unless it is made explicit.
- Find every opportunity to share appreciation, especially to seniors and managers in the team.

- Make it a habit to assist a colleague either with improving their skill or improving the quality of their work.

AS A LEADER

- Be sensitive to individuals and team members who need support and are struggling to make a mark.
- Recognize potential non-core skills which complement the core skills in the team.
- Encourage forums where the big picture and end-to-end context of the team can be discussed.
- Drive open discussions on constraints involved and solicit improvement ideas.
- Explain the value being delivered by the team and often engage in future road map discussions.

#StickyNoteWorthy

It is literally true that you can succeed best and quickest by helping others to succeed.

Napoleon Hill

Good leaders and successful individuals at work are the ones who appreciate this aspect of 'enabling others' instead of getting fixated on their individual constraints and move ahead with due recognition and success. Also, Gopal's story illustrates the moral that each individual has something unique to offer. Sometimes it is obvious, and sometimes it needs effort to be discovered. One should not give up or be too self-critical during the process of this discovery of 'fitting in'.

5 VOLLEYING NICELY

Sometimes an insight dawns on you, rather gets thrown at you, in most unexpected places and times. The following one was at a breakfast table in ibis Schiphol Amsterdam during one of my work travels. I was in a rush to take the shuttle to office with just under 20 minutes to finish my breakfast. The room was buzzing with people and several children in what looked like a sports uniform adding to the liveliness. I manoeuvred through the children as I filled my tray and scanned the tables to find a place to settle down.

'I have my reflections on the game yesterday, Sara, and they are not all bad, don't worry,' came a rough voice from an adjacent table. By the looks of it, I related it to a middle-aged man with a heavy build, occupying almost two chairs on one side of the table and addressing a lady and another young guy, both dressed in the same sports uniform as the kids. 'We were so close coach; we lost in the last few minutes,' said Sara. 'By one point,' said the guy sitting next to Sara. 'Yeah! The team was so busy playing, with each player focusing on the moves but not playing together,' said the coach, 'except for Jenny,' he added.

Two kids crossed this table and greeted their coaches as they carried their breakfast tray looking for a table to sit. 'Jenny is not the most skilful player of all, but the way she played—she played with a lot of heart! She does not show tiredness, keeps encouraging her teammates and gives more than 100 per cent. You should encourage this trait in the other kids without judging any of them,' said the coach. 'I was expecting Peter to score some more points than he did; he showed so much promise in practice games,' said the other guy. 'That's the thing, Johan; he was trying hard to score but not play with the rest. Either he was scoring or missing; it's largely a team game the last time I checked, isn't it?' coughed the coach as he spoke gulping down whatever a deep slurp of coffee he could draw from his cup.

'Did you observe the team dynamics? Not so long into the game, the team started working as a unit with Jenny as the main player, whereas with Peter it wasn't seamless; no one was willing even to pass the ball to him, even though he was close to receive the pass and score,' said the coach.

'Agree, 70 per cent of the points were influenced by Jenny and team working together. Like us, even the team was banking on Peter as the strongest player to score,' said Sara. 'Which he is; each time he had the ball in his "zone", his smashes were accurate, and he scored,' added the coach, 'But when he couldn't do that, he wasn't being so effective with the rest of the team and they reciprocated,' he laughed.

'But don't forget, these are kids we are talking about, and it is important that they not only enjoy the game but also get some of these important aspects into their core playing culture,' he smiled. 'I am pretty sure these observations are not just for the kids, coach,' said Johan winking at Sara. She nodded in reply.

'Tell them in the language that they can understand, Sara and Johan—"be competitive but have fun" and "practise passing the ball more than smashing it back". Most times giving a nice volley to another player creates a better chance of scoring, doesn't it?' he smiled. 'I remember from my training days, the practice started with using half the court practising passes to each other before we started using the full court for a real game.'

'But isn't winning important, coach? Some of them quickly lose motivation unless they win a few games,' asked Sara.

'Hmm, now I will give you perhaps an old-fashioned reply that I received from my senior coach who trained me a while ago; it was…,' said the coach as he took a sip of coffee (this is the third filling from when I started following their conversation, I observed cheekily). 'These kids come to you to discover the best of themselves via the sport, Anders; winning or losing should aid that process of discovery, and that is your biggest job as a coach…,' he said and added, 'Of course, it applies to any other field….'

Sara rolled her eyes, 'Got to prepare for the next match,' she picked up her tray. 'Not easy, but we gotta try—keep them together. Playing volleyball is learning as much playing with your team as much as it is scoring against the opposing team, but you know that, don't you?' said Anders.

'Priceless', I thought as I recollected the conversation summary on the way to office: '(a) busy playing but not playing with each other well, (b) playing with a lot of heart and charging up others vs display of skill (being the brightest in the lot) but not being a team player, (c) no matter the off-field strategy, the team organizes (plays around) itself around smaller cohesive units of players working well with each other, (d) learning the right language to coach the team, without judging anyone and (e) not losing focus on the "process of discovery" (and the sport as well as the outcomes as a means to it)'.

As I focused my thoughts on the upcoming discussions in the office themed around 'ecosystem play', I could not help appreciating the relevance of points stated above and their applicability in the day-to-day interactions.

#WorkplaceWhispers

I recorded the above incident in one of my work travels to Amsterdam. This narrative provides insights into how a team shapes itself up progressively and performs together (or otherwise).

A typical challenge faced by a leader (either as a coach or as a lead player) is when some of the individuals do not play (apply themselves) fully and remain guarded. This makes it difficult to sense the interpersonal dynamics and make the right adjustments. Sports offer a great insight and solution towards this as well. The environment of 'having fun' (and not being judged) allows individuals to drop their guard and participate better, and nurturing such an environment should be a constant endeavour of leadership.

'TOO BUSY PLAYING THAT GOAL IS FORGOTTEN'

It is not uncommon, especially in long-running programmes or projects, that the team gets so busy working that they forget the purpose of the programme. The focus shifts to meeting near-term deadlines, being green on the KPIs and surviving the day, rather than pausing often to check if the team as a whole is on the right track.

Staying excited in the goal and remembering it often are essential to avoid the trap of short-term milestones or getting exhausted with day-to-day problems.

'WE PLAY WELL WITH FRIENDS AT WORK–LOCATION DOESN'T MATTER'

A global delivery manager from TCS and one of my good friends, Phani Vellanki, says, 'While models and frameworks help define operating structures and nudge people to interact with each other in a specified frame, real interactions/insight sharing happen between friends at work.'

It is important to create that kind of an environment where information is pushed freely rather than pulled formally via extensive reporting. If the dominant behaviours in a team are wrought with formality, seriousness, rush and lack of appreciation, teams tend to stay guarded, play for themselves and eventually lose interest.

#Do you recognize the need for this element of having 'friends at work' and can you think of a few initiatives which can sustain good behaviours?

TEAMWORK IS CRUCIAL FOR CARE

'Teamwork is crucial to better take care of the patients, and we should all put effort in a coordinated and concerted way to get the best outcome for the patients. Key to any successful execution of a plan (a surgery) is taking everybody on board,' says Dr Kesava Mannur, a leading London-based bariatric and gastrointestinal consulting surgeon.

#GameofDrones

AS AN INDIVIDUAL

- I just joined this team which is apparently executing this programme for the past one year; I have no clue what the ambition is, I just keep to my assigned work.
- I am part of a large team; I interact formally with a lot of people, but I have my own mini circle of friends; we speak the same language anyway, so it's easy to connect.
- I am tolerant to this mini group only, and we tend to appreciate each other, but not so much with others.

- I have so much work to do that I don't remember when I actually helped someone else in the team, well not many helped me so far.
- I update a weekly status report; I don't know frankly what someone can make sense out of it; I just fill it for compliance. Somebody needs to talk to me to really understand what I am doing.

AS A LEADER

- I am in a cycle of deliverables and things to do—month on month/quarter on quarter—with absolutely no time to connect with the team.
- We work on making programme charters, vision and plan once a year, but we do not refer to it again; the programme takes its own course.
- I do not get the time to focus on team dynamics, how they are organizing themselves in reality—there is an operating structure, and I expect that everyone aligns to that one.
- It is important to have fun, so we have made it part of the process; we meet once every week on a specified time and try to have fun.

Now discover and evaluate each roadblock. Think of it as a real drone and see how it is doing. Be honest and review how well you are flying it.

☐ **Fully autonomous flight**

☐ **Guided flights**

☐ **Irregular flight path**

☐ **Unwilling to take off**

#KeyResonatingActions

AS A TEAM PLAYER

- Be unrelenting until you fully understand the background and context of the programme (or the goals of the team).
- Try to understand the current operating structure—team roles—and how it has changed over a period and what influenced this change; this will give you a good insight into the activities and goals of the team.
- Learn the practices of the team—both on work and off work (if any) and participate fully.
- Appreciate enthusiasm and individuals who walk an extra mile to bring it forth.
- Share freely (subject to confidentiality and role of recipients); encouraging flow is a terrific way to improve team spirit.
- In your own way, make it a habit to assist a colleague (if no one needs assistance, see how you can help with further improving someone's work)—lending a hand is a key resonating behaviour which will sustain a team.
- Being part of a subgroup is natural, but be generally open to everyone in the team.

AS A LEADER

- Make work enjoyable, without sacrificing compliance—encourage those who can help with this aspect.
- Meet often to remind the team of the goals and if the current measures are helping, stay on the course (or otherwise).
- Pay attention to the team dynamics—if there are subgroups, try to be a common friend of all.

- Sometimes be a coach, but try to be a player too who the team can interact with in the field, or else team will not have empathy to the leadership decisions.
- Tirelessly identify collaborators and make them feel valuable. They are the real assets to keep the team going.

#StickyNoteWorthy

You don't win or lose the games because of the 11 (players) you select. You win or lose with what those 11 do on the field.

Rahul Dravid

Everyone understands that teamwork is important and playing together is healthier than playing alone. However, when it comes to execution, not all teams manage to live this understanding, and those who manage to do stand apart. Being tolerant with each other, willing to experiment and trying to enjoy the game day after day help to find the right interpersonal play, but more than anything else, coming to the game daily to play counts the most.

6

ONE SHOT, A LIFETIME OF PRACTICE

Facing Disruptions with Persistence

The king of Himapura lost his eldest son in the battle with *the beast*. The beast also left the kingdom in tatters and went back into the deep forests in the mountains which surrounded Himapura. Legend has it that one of the ancestors of the kingdom, Surasena, was so blinded by his might that in his arrogance he humiliated an ascetic. The ascetic cursed him to be a beast, 'Your might blinded you king; you think you are entitled to do whatever you want. You have forgotten the values of humility, respect and simplicity. So be it, I curse you to disrupt the might of your kingdom every 20 years. The known means of training of which you are so proud of will come to no avail to your people and your armies.' Surasena pleaded to forgive him and provide a way out of the curse to which the ascetic said, 'If someone from your family lets go of his identity and develops the needed virtues to fight the beast, the curse will break.' And so it was, for generations the curse consumed the heirs of Himapura and no matter how hard they tried, the entire might of the Himapura could not conquer the beast.

King Surendra was distraught and enraged. His eldest son, Ajaya, who was barely 22 years old and yet one of the finest warriors of Himapura accepted the challenge and died in the hands of the beast without a fight. Guha, the family teacher, advised Surendra to send away Vikram with him to be trained differently. 'The curse would break if only Vikram grew up not as a royal but as a man on his own and trained unconventionally. The beast cannot be conquered by any known weapon or means, but if I can train Vikram to gain strength and forge his own weapon, there may be a chance.' But similar to his predecessors, the king was unwilling to let go. He decided to save his second son, the two-year-old, and send him away to his uncle in a neighbouring kingdom. He would take on the beast and die, and there will not be any more for the beast left from the royal blood in Himapura to kill.

Soma, the trusted servant, instead took Vikram to the teacher Guha and told him the king's predicament. Guha was a master in the art of wielding weapons and warfare and ran his gurukul (the residential school run by masters in olden times to teach students various arts, including the art of wielding weapons and warfare) to train students into warriors for Himapura. 'So be it! I will bring up Vikram like a common child and will train him into a fierce warrior, but he needs to *earn his worthiness* or he too will perish in the hands of the beast. You leave the kingdom and do not return until 20 years have passed,' so saying Guha bid farewell to Soma.

Guha renamed Vikram to Vijaya and brought him up as his own son. He told the rest of the students in his gurukul that he found Vijaya in the forest and some poor mother would have forsaken her child. As Vijaya grew up in the gurukul amid the training arena watching other students (warriors) practise the art of war, he took a keen liking to archery. Although still a young kid of six years, nothing impressed Vijaya more than seeing some of the best students pierce the most difficult targets and shoot arrows the farthest. 'When can I start learning to practise, master?' asked the little Vijaya. 'In time, my son, before that you should build strength, practise bending this staff. The day you do that I will start training you in archery,' smiled Guha and gave him a tough looking staff which was dark, stout and long. 'It's very heavy,' Vijaya tried to hold on to the staff as he wanted to show that he was up for the challenge. Over the next several years, whenever Vijaya went to his master asking for permission to practise archery, he would get the same question: 'How much can you bend the stick?' Vijaya could barely bend it, try as hard as he might. He trusted his master and worked on this strange piece of wood as he watched other students practise in the arena. 'Why are you always going around with that strange stick?' other students ridiculed him. 'Does the master want to train you as a shepherd?' they smirked. 'No,' cried Vijaya, 'I will be the best archer of all,' he replied with determination and applied some more force on the stick, but it would not relent.

Guha also taught Vijaya the art of making a bow and made him create several types of bows for the practice of the warriors. He taught Vijaya to identify the right tree—what characteristics to look for and how to gently carve out the bow. 'If the wood is too hard, the bow will snap and if it is too supple, it will not shoot an impactful arrow,' advised Guha.

As two more years went by, Vijaya learnt the art of identifying trees and making good bows. However, he did not give up working on the staff, and he did not lose patience. 'Now we know what the master would want to make of you, you poor servant boy; he wants you to assist him in running this place, you "bow-maker,"' ridiculed the students. Although it hurt, Vijaya ignored them and he somehow had a firm belief in his master.

At last, one day, with all his might that a 16-year-old could muster, he bent the staff into a beautiful curve. He ran to his master to showcase his achievement. 'Indeed! This is remarkable; now you are ready to start practising archery,' stated Guha. 'Now that you have learnt to bend your bow, why don't you carve it fully and string it up,' smiled Guha to the utter joy of Vijaya. 'All along I was holding on to my bow? I knew there was something behind this exercise master; I am thankful to you. Please teach me to hit the most difficult targets without missing them,' asked an enthused Vijaya bubbling with energy. 'Son! You have earned the trust of your bow by being with it, working on it but never ridiculing it. Respect for the means you have is the first sign of worthiness. Now I will train you to shoot arrows, but it will not be conventional. Are you willing to trust me once again?' looked Guha enquiringly. 'I will, master; let us begin.'

The next day, Guha took Vijaya to the bottom of the mountain by name Silavarsha (raining rocks). The mountain had great slopes and still looked fresh from the volcanic eruption which formed it several hundred years ago. The boulders on the mountain continuously rolled down into the valley, giving the mountain its name. 'Listen carefully, Vijaya! This training may kill you, but if you show enough courage and practice with all your focus, you will be the best archer that you have always wanted to be,' Guha spoke reassuringly. 'I am ready, master; what should I do?' 'You will stand at the foot of Silavarsha and wait for the boulders to roll down, and when you see one rolling down, you will charge towards it shooting arrows at it. Your task will be to smash the boulders with your arrows and when you do that, you would have been trained,' finished Guha. Vijaya was distraught. Surely this was not what he ever saw in the gurukul! Even the worst of Guha's students were not trained to this degree of extremity. 'Maybe there is something in it for me. Besides, I am starting so late and would never catch up to the skills of the others if I tried to do what they did. Alas! I thought archery was about piercing the finest and most intricate targets, but this seems to be a test of my courage and strength,' Vijaya paused as he tried to prepare himself for the challenge. 'Vijaya, remember if you do not get out of the way in time, you will be certainly killed by the incoming boulder; be quick to decide and *use your courage wisely*,' warned Guha.

This was an impossible task. The first six months, Vijaya barely managed to get out of the rushing boulders. let alone stringing up an arrow to shoot them. However, his teacher kept guiding him. 'Shooting a stationery object would do you no good, Vijaya; continue to practise. Look for the shot which will stall the boulder and smash it!' Guha told his pupil firmly.

Vijaya continued to practise shooting arrows at the rolling rocks and mounds of sediment and gradually picked up the strength and agility needed in his legs *to get to the state of poise while in motion*. His focus became so good that he lost himself completely; all he could see was the area of the rock where he should land the next arrow and the rest of his body supported his aim.

Vijaya continued to get taunted by the other warriors often and they even enticed him to duels to show their skills. 'You seem to be developing the muscle of a labourer, "rock shooter", but how good is your archery? Shall we have a competition?' they tried to tease him. 'I know I am not good at what you do, but I believe that I am good at what I do. The one thing that I can do, none of you can and I will work further on it,' Vijaya replied calmly. 'He must be born of a shepherd for sure; if he was a true warrior, he would get enraged and fight with us! He doesn't even offer us a chance to beat him up,' they laughed behind him.

Guha also observed that Bharani (the ironwood tree) issued its powerful branches indicating that the time was near. He called out to Vijaya and took him to the tree. Vijaya observed that the bow he had was of the same colour as this tree and understood that the wood came from this tree. He wondered why his master never took him to this tree before. 'Vijaya, do you see that sturdy branch over there? What do you think of it?' asked Guha. 'It is magnificent! I can carve a worthy bow which a great warrior of your gurukul can adorn, master,' humbly replied Vijaya. '*I am very pleased with your humility*; please attempt to separate the branch and start crafting the bow,' ordered Guha. Vijaya was elated, 'There must be a warrior in the gurukul indeed who I will have the great fortune to present this bow to!' he thought. It took huge effort from Vijaya to separate the branch and even more effort to carve the bow from the branch. After several months of effort, a magnificent bow was carved by Vijaya. Guha asked him to prepare tough cords made of twined fibre from the toughest bamboo and roots of other trees of the forest. 'You know that a mighty bow would need…', 'the strongest string, yes master', Vjiaya was up for the task.

'An arrow released from this bow can even blast rocks, master; who did you choose to present this powerful weapon to?' asked Vijaya in front of the warriors that Guha asked to assemble the next day.

Guha smiled and addressed all his students, 'This bow has been carved out from the legendary Bharani tree. Only the mightiest of warriors could wield it and face the beast which will awaken from its slumber soon. Which of you would like to take up the challenge?' asked Guha. Several courageous warriors came forth and said, 'Master! We do not fear the beast as it would not fight anyone but the royalty; we would like to try to wield this bow.' 'Very well, try to string it up with the chord which Vijaya has prepared and shoot an arrow,' Guha encouraged them. The warriors took turns to lift the bow which did not look very stout but was extremely heavy. It was impossible for them to even bend it slightly. 'From where does it gather so much weight and resistance!' they thought. Vijaya was watching with glee to see the spectacle of the greatest warrior stepping forth and wielding this weapon. But as every one of the warriors failed, Vijaya was also disappointed. 'Is there no one in this gurukul who could make my master proud? I am not even a good shot, else I could have tried,' he told himself.

'Step forth, Vikram, the prince of Himapura!' announced Guha addressing Vijaya. 'The time has come for you to know who you really are and face your destiny.' The warriors in the gurukul were astonished to hear the story of Vijaya and his true identity. Vikram, however, felt sad to hear the story of his ancestors and the sacrifice of his father to keep him alive. 'We are indebted forever to you, master, for having prepared me to meet the purpose of my life. Now I know why I have not trained the way others did and prepared all my life for that one shot which will lift the curse from my family,' Vikram stated courageously as he bent the bow and strung it up with determination and ease. As he finished preparing the bow, there was a deafening cry from deep within the forest as if a huge thunder exploded in the sky. 'I am ready,' said Vikram as he pulled the cord of his bow to make a vibrant sound from the bow of Bharani.

The beast rolled through the forest smashing trees and rocks along the way as if the biggest boulder of the mountain came rolling down. Vikram waited patiently at the bottom of the mountain with a smile on his face. As the huge boulder (beast) came charging towards him, he gently picked up an arrow made from the Bharani tree from his quiver, 'This is what you trained me for,' he thought. He poised his stance firmly and made a deep draw on his bow so much so that for an onlooker he appeared one with the bow itself. He lost sight of the surroundings and himself as his sight focused on the spot which should be pierced by his arrow and as the beast came within the shooting range, he released the arrow like a thunderbolt hitting a dead tree. There was a booming sound, like that of a mountain cracking up into pieces. The beast smashed hard into the ground with roaring cries in pain and breathed its last.

Guha opened his eyes as he concluded his morning meditation and smiling to his students said, 'The curse has been lifted; send word to the king that the prince is ready to return to the palace!'

The upward spiral of 'technology' and the 'evolving needs of the market' have ensured that change/disruption is the norm, with constantly evolving and disappearing business models and their influence on the entire value chain. This is driving organizations to orient themselves culturally as learning organizations open to change and nimble enough to adapt quickly (with due consideration to their USPs). At an individual level, there is a calling to be *adaptable* and *persistent* with one's learning, and not be trapped by the comfort of entitlement.

ENTITLEMENT AND DISRUPTION

Are the two common facets of workplace(s) with untoward outcomes usually going hand in hand in a subtle way? *Disruption* follows someone (or a unit) who gets comfortable with *entitlement* and stops putting in the needed effort.

Devendar Reddy, an executive in an oil and gas company, was interviewing Balasarada for a leadership role in his unit. After about an hour of discussion, he confirmed that he was happy to welcome her into his group. Balasarada expressed her hesitation that after listening to the expectations, she might not be ready to take on such a hefty role. Devendar said, 'I am happy you have mentioned this with honesty. This is an important observation. When we elevate or recruit an associate into a role, we do it based on their mettle but more importantly on their potential. But it usually takes several months to couple of years, depending upon the scope and seniority of the role, the calibre of the associate in understanding the various aspects involved and the effort which the associate is willing to put in. As long as you are willing to learn, you are good, and we will be with you.' That wise counsel helped Sarada to be watchful and not fall prey to the trap of entitlement—'I am ready; I deserve to be here' and rather work with 'This is a beginning; I need to fill into the role by putting in needed effort.'

MULTIPLE FACETS OF DISRUPTION

Disruption doesn't always show itself in tangible ways. At least it would be easier to sense it if it does so. More serious and subtle kind of disruption which one needs to be aware of is the one caused by denial that everything is okay or will get sorted on its own. It happens slowly and erodes the status quo over a period.

'Investing time in relationships and learning is a necessity for a leader. Failure with the former would lead to loss of loyalty from the team or stakeholders, and failure with the latter would lead to erosion of one's capability to lead over a period. One should be wary of both these disruptive tendencies,' says Nrusimha Kiran, Head of Sales and Strategy for Siri AB.

GROWING WITH THE PACE OF CHANGE

Each one of us has an ability to deal with change to varying degrees. It takes an element of courage and dispassion to let go of current area of work and the associated position which comes with it and start afresh in a new area. Some associates though seem to flourish each time a change hits them, as if they are hardwired to be driven by change. They are not too many in number and are in high demand as management tends to rely on them repeatedly.

Of course, not all fields are the same, and 'change' doesn't mean moving multiple areas but investing in lifelong learning and practice. 'All our life we learn and what appears best at this time may not be right with new evidence or experience. We have moved on from open surgery to keyhole surgery (laparoscopic) and now to robotic surgery. We have to take up new things as we get to know them better, and this requires an orientation to continuous learning without any inhibition. To succeed with new learning, it is important to have your fundamentals strong, and that one keeps practising', says Dr Kesava Mannur, a leading consulting surgeon based out of London who established the bariatric surgical unit at Homerton University Hospital, London, in 2003 and developed this into one of the leading reputed centres in bariatric surgery in the UK.

#GameofDrones

- I am in constant fear that I might lose my job as my management might think this is not an important role.
- I am constantly looking for which projects I should get into or tools I must learn and pay less attention to my current project work.
- I am working with the best-in-class product out there in my domain and feel sad for the others who are not in my project, as this is the place to be.
- For me, my area of work is like religion and I cannot let go of it. I am champion of my technology and try to solve every problem with this.
- Now that I am in this role which is hefty, I think I will get undivided attention and support from the team.
- I do not pay attention to the macro changes in my domain/area of work.
- I cannot aspire for next-level roles as I don't have connections with my management. I think only those who are closely connected with leadership team tend to get promoted.

Now discover and evaluate each roadblock. Think of it as a real drone and see how it is doing. Be honest and review how well you are flying it.

- [ ] **Fully autonomous flight**
- [ ] **Guided flights**
- [ ] **Irregular flight path**
- [ ] **Unwilling to take off**

#KeyResonatingActions

- Identify the 'minimum expectations' and 'maximum potential' which can be derived from your role. Have an impossible problem/aspiration in your role which you can attempt and solve.
- Appreciate your current opportunity, no matter what job role you may be performing; look for on-the-job learning and ways to bring in innovation.
- Trace every activity which is performed back to its fundamentals and work with a mentor to understand the reason behind the procedures/process at your workplace or domain.
- Be observant of change in your industry and embrace new learning opportunities.
- Try to draw lessons from both failures and successes at work or from your learning attempts.
- Be persistent with taking feedback, encourage people to appreciate what you are doing right and improve it further.
- Have at least one expert (or someone who can teach you more than you know in your current area of work) to mentor you constantly.

#StickyNoteWorthy

Without your involvement you can't succeed. With your involvement you can't fail.

Dr A. P. J. Abdul Kalam

A good understanding of the 'jobs being done' as discussed by Professor Clayton Christensen in Theory of Jobs To Be Done helps one appreciate the relevance and effectiveness of the work being done (or roles being played) in fulfilling a need of the customer. This understanding makes it possible to stay focused on the value being delivered, rather than getting stuck on the means (which usually get disrupted when needs change or evolve). When the focus remains on constantly sustaining or improving the value delivered, there is inherent learning daily, and even failures will be seen as essential lessons. When applied at a team level, it will lead to self-imposed disruption aka innovation, and entitlement finds no place in such a culture.

7 SURVIVING FIRE, ENRICHING OTHERS

Tommy was a sprightly man in his early 70s, but he looked like he barely crossed 50. He was strong and tough and as swift as a young bear moving through the forest. 'Lived all my life in the woods. When I was young, I bought a piece of land in the Tiveden National Forest and built a cabin for myself; forest has everything, and I didn't have a need to venture out.' After living there for several years, he moved slightly outside to the edge of the national forest, built a larger home and lives there along with his eight wolf dogs.

'I have learnt carpentry; I love working with good wood. I do small chores for the national forest authorities here and help the neighbours with broken stuff. See I built those…,' said he as he showed around the small structures which he built to provide directions to the forest hikers and the cabin he built at the base station of the Tiveden National Forest. 'I can tell good wood just by looking at it; it talks to me,' he laughed looking at the trees as if talking to his brothers.

'No good wood these days, too much cutting down, too soon,' he said sadly. 'In my younger days, if we wanted wood, we used to approach the tree very humbly like this…,' he stooped down straining his knees and walked like a prowling tiger about to pounce on its prey, 'and asked "dear tree, I need your wood to make my window; can I please take a branch from you?"' 'Of course, the tree always wants to help, asking nicely makes it feel good and we only take what we want,' he quickly added.

'Look at these trees; they are hundreds of years old, and do you know why?' he paused with a wise frown. 'Look closer; do you see the charred wood? It's like a trophy for the tree—because it survived forest fire! A tree which survives forest fire generates the strongest wood and can live longer than any other tree. Fire can be good for the forest. It clears down the forest by burning the weeds, moss and lichen and creates space for the big trees.'

'But what if the entire tree gets burnt down?' someone asked. 'Living tree carries water, even in hot summer, and at most it gets charred. Even otherwise, as long as the root system is intact, a better tree grows up. Don't worry, fire is good! I have seen at least four fires in my lifetime burning down the entire parts of the forest, but what comes back next is beautiful and fresh,' he smiled at our puzzled faces.

After the governments started controlling the forests, we stopped having natural fire and we see trees like those,' he pointed to a tree which seemed like it broke on its own weight. 'See the trunk, so thin; do you observe anything else? Hmmm … compare with this strong tree … see anything?' he paused again. 'Ah! You city people, do not worry, I will tell you. That tree has lesser branches; it grew too fast too soon. And look around it; it is almost alone.'

'A strong tree grows on its own pace, with a lot of branches, and as it grows more branches, it gathers more thickness around its trunk. It attracts more animals, more shrubbery, and as if it communicates with other trees underground, it helps other trees get healthier. Does it sound like garbage? I am not an educated man, but I see this all the time!' he tried to explain.

'These days, I see a lot of plantation by private owners; they chop off the branches quickly so that the trees can grow fast and more wood can be generated! These plantations are mini wood factories. Here, let me show you; there you see that patch? Lone trees waiting to be cut down. No animals or birds come around there! It is sad. You want to grow alone and fall under your own weight, so sad!' he looked away as if to avoid looking at a horror scene.

'If we walk further up a mile, you will see natural trees and undisturbed forest bed. Every strong tree has so much weight that it carries as it grows. The big birds also like to nest on these trees. These trees almost feel like they are selfless; they grow as if…', he paused again to show respect, '…with a lot of responsibility', he smiled to himself.

'You see this green moss like thing under the rocks; you can eat it if you get lost in the forest; don't tell anyone I told you that … hehehe, you are not supposed to disturb the forest….' As he continued to speak about various animal species, how to make a bird cry and understand if a tree is not well, he gave us an impression of being the old guard of the forest who has found a deep connection with the ecosystem. His knowledge of the forest perhaps if formalized would have earned him a doctorate and he could have been a celebrated professor of the continent. None of that mattered to Tommy.

#WorkplaceWhispers

The relevance of leadership in the workplace and the importance of grooming/developing leaders are widely recognized facts in the industry. The facets of leadership are as diverse as the fields in which they are applied, and there is a lot of inspiration which one can gather by being a discerning student and learning from day-to-day experiences both at work and off work. The narrative of Tommy brings forth certain fundamental elements of leadership which have very practical implications for a workplace.

TENACITY IS THE NAME OF THE GAME

'For me, it is one word—tenacity!' says Shanker Mishra, my good friend and a global delivery manager. 'All leadership development happens when faced with tough challenges, and a leader should be tenacious in not giving up, keeping a steady focus and powering ahead day after day. Eventually, the problems fall in line,' he adds.

NOT GIVING UP ON THE TEAM

Here is a fond recollection of an incident from Bhawani (name changed), a network engineer from a company based out of North America. 'It was my initial months in the organization. It was late evening, and I could hear the frustrated keystrokes of my computer resoundingly in the almost empty zone. I was trying hard to fix a problem with my code. My project leader had this habit of taking a quick round to ensure that everybody left before he left for the day and he came by to check why I was still around. I told him that I wanted to fix the issue in time for the batch compile the next day. He sat along with me with a broad smile, giving gentle nudges on how to understand the problem, but without solving it. Neither did he give up on me and dropped the solution, nor did he give up on himself. He kept saying that this is a great opportunity to learn an important lesson and encouraged me to read the compile errors (errors being thrown by the system when there is something wrong with the software written) over and over again. It took until 3 AM in the morning before I could successfully compile the code. He then dropped me home on his scooter before leaving to his.'

GROWING TOGETHER: TAKING THE TEAM ALONG

One of the fantastic leaders who I worked with, Keshav Varma, a senior business leader, displayed this quality of consistently taking the team along and giving them first-hand exposure and visibility. He would go to great lengths to get a few of us a seat at the table in executive connects with customers, or important strategic meetings, where we would see him in action and learn from the interactions. He would then encourage us to collectively reflect on how the interactions went and what we (mentally) noted. 'The best way to grow is to focus on the growth of your team, and giving exposure and visibility to them is a good approach to achieve that,' he would often remark.

MISSION: LETTING GO–HOLDING ON

Kingshuk Chatterjee had been sent on a mission: to fix the quality issues with the network and IT operations of the Asia-Pacific (APAC) region of a telecom major. The customer complaints were at an all-time peak, and the telco was at a risk of losing customers if they did not act fast. Several leaders tried to bring this region back on track but failed, and Kingshuk was chosen to do this task, given his seniority and process expertise. 'I have been sent here to drive process excellence, fix quality issues, bring in a good delivery rhythm, restore customer confidence and set the operations on the right track. I have been asked to achieve all of this in the next two years. But my personal target is to take us to success in one year after which I will move on. I also have the name of my successor written down on a piece of paper in this envelope, and when we celebrate success by the end of the year from now, I will announce the name and hand this region over to that individual,' Kingshuk addressed the subregional heads. With Kingshuk's drive, expertise and positive leadership, the region became a flagship unit within 18 months and went from being a region which no one in their right mind will go to work with in the company to a region where one should work at least once in their career. This was a great display of leadership where the leader took on all the pain and effort to prepare a better ground and hand it over to another one.

#As a leader, it is worth reflecting on these three questions often: What is your mission? What are you holding on to? And what are you constantly letting go?

WATCH OUT: SUBCONSCIOUS EMULATION

Teams constantly look at and emulate the behaviours of the leader. A nervous leader drives nervousness in the team and a cheerful/confident leader drives confidence. In the example given above, the message to the account leadership was resonating with confidence and in a way fostering a positive outcome: 'We will have a success meet where I will announce my successor.' This set the entire team to work with a positive frame of mind, but also 'in less than a year's time'—a time-bound affirmative drive!

POLITICALLY CHARGED...

Here is another experience where clear advice and support from the leader provided guidance and direction at a time when I needed it the most.

I was to lead a programme overseas, in North America, and the customer was facing a difficult business situation. The environment was rife with political agendas and people were driven by a sense of insecurity. Within a couple of months after I started work in the geography, I was at my wits' end and wondered how anything constructive could be done in an environment where everything seemed to be going downhill.

Our SVP and BU Head V. Rajanna was visiting the geography at that point to meet the customers. When he was meeting the TCS team briefly over lunch, I brought up what was on my mind. 'Technology, requirements and solutioning are not the problems, but in this very political environment, everyone is driving their own agenda and pushing us in different directions. I am worried that we will end up upsetting someone or the other, even as we do the right thing,' I complained to Rajanna. His advice was, 'Where there are people under stress, there is bound to be some politics. Always keep your message consistent and honest, with everyone. They may get upset initially, but they will appreciate it eventually. Also remember that while it is okay not to be in front of the customer when they are happy with you, ensure that you are in front of them when they are upset with you and face the challenges head on. Keep doing the right thing for the customers and TCS; we will support you.'

#GameofDrones

- I tend to keep the team away from important meetings and take all the information from them and attend the meetings myself.
- I prefer tight control on the team at all times.
- I do not take personal interest in their lives nor their background.
- While I talk about ownership within my team, I am usually suspicious and feel insecure sometimes.
- I do not spend time checking the empowerment needed for the team to take decisions and move things forward; they can come to me for that.

- I prefer rules over values.
- I tend to focus more on personal growth and the next big milestone ahead of me and think about team's growth occasionally.
- I end up pulling inputs and information most of the times from the team than getting it from them proactively.
- I constantly believe that I need to push more discipline in my team.
- I rather want my team to think that I am intelligent and sharp than kind and cheerful.
- I enjoy putting people on the spot in meetings and providing incisive feedback.
- I have done sometimes double-digit reviews on the same deliverable to make the team uplift their quality of work and get it to a shape that I see fit.

Now discover and evaluate each roadblock. Think of it as a real drone and see how it is doing. Be honest and review how well you are flying it.

☐ **Fully autonomous flight**

☐ **Guided flights**

☐ **Irregular flight path**

☐ **Unwilling to take off**

#KeyResonatingActions

- Surprise associates with kindness—indulge in proactive acts of empathetic leadership to gain the trust of associates.
- Build a reputation of being a 'giving leader'.

- Be approachable, especially during tough times or when someone in the team makes a mistake.
- Providing feedback need not be an insult-prone experience to the team.
- Be willing to listen to the team, even if the problems being discussed cannot be solved easily.
- Provide specific, elaborate and genuine appreciation.
- Practise a healthy say/do ratio; this will automatically drive seriousness in the team.
- Provide visibility to the team by giving them access to forums and people which they would not have otherwise.
- Show interest in the work done by the associates of the team; try to know what a typical workday in their life looks like.
- Show more than tell. Working together is a better way than providing feedback multiple times and getting into a long *feedback/implement/review/feedback/implement* cycle.

#StickyNoteWorthy

The growth and development of people is the highest calling of leadership.

Harvey Firestone

A robust belief (roots) system, integrity and constant practice of looking at the big picture (growing others) are noble attributes of good leaders. Even when they get tough, it is only to encourage fine-pruning of others for their growth. And like big trees which attract birds and animals, individuals naturally tend to flock to them.

Constantly spending time in narrating the values of the organization (or values in general as applicable to one's work) and helping the team empathize with the big picture help in strengthening the roots of the leader as well as those of the entire team. Every individual is constantly striving, consciously or otherwise, to answer the question 'Am I making a difference?' and this is a great opportunity for a leader to connect at the deepest level with every individual of the team and in the process build a healthy workplace.

8

BEYOND THE SHELL

Once upon a time, in a mystical forest lived a turtle by name Figet. No one knew how old Figet was, and the animals sure did think that Figet was at least a few hundred years old, but there was no way to find out. Figet was supposed to be magical and could speak with animals and humans too! He roamed the forest and was found by those in need of advice or desperate help. He had one mysterious problem though—he was very shy and forgetful. His power of knowledge was bestowed only when the creature seeking help could make him remember who he was and earned Figet's trust. No one knew how to do this, although there were random stories of how Figet saved the day when there was trouble.

'Tell me, Rabbit, how did you get him to talk to you?' roared Bernard, the lion king. 'I d.d.d.d.don't know, sire! My family was very hungry, and we hadn't eaten for days and Figet appeared from nowhere. I j.j.j.j.just told him that we are scared and need help,' said Mr Rabbit. 'You are lying, is that it? Figet doesn't speak easy; tell me exactly what you said,' demanded Bernard. 'S.s.s.s.si..si..sire,' stuttered the scared Rabbit. 'Oh stop that and speak clean or I will eat you,' Bernard grew impatient.

'I j.j.just, no, it was he, he s.s.said that he was scared too and asked where he was. I told him that he was safe with us and there was nothing to be worried about. And then I told him that we had heard several stories about him and how he was wise and powerful,' paused Rabbit trying to catch his breath.

'Then what?' asked Bernard. 'Then, s.s.sire, he slowly got his head to the entrance of his huge shell and said he had no friends. My children told him that we could be his friends and we would keep him happy. He smiled and brought his head out completely. He then asked what our worry was. We asked for some food,' concluded Rabbit. 'The great Figet shows up and you just ask for carrots??? You fool,' thundered Bernard. 'Get out of my sight before I snack you out.'

The lion king wanted to grab hold of Figet and become more powerful. 'Your ancestors got the counsel of Figet when there was great famine in the mystical forest, O king!' said Cunny, the jackal minister. 'I heard that before, but I need to know how to make him appear first and then I will ask him to give me powers, make me immortal,' Bernard growled. 'Unless you show that you have a genuine need, Figet won't appear; you need to speak humble, sire,' Cunny lowered his voice not to upset the lion, 'And each time he appears, his memory gets reset; get him out of his shell completely, sire, and you will be bestowed with what you want!' 'Stop your sermon! I know all that! He has been last sighted beside the jingle brooks; I am headed that way now,' Bernard hurried to the brook.

'Oh, I am in distress! I wish I had someone to help me,' Bernard started to make loud wails and the smaller suspecting animals ran away looking at this. 'I may die now if I don't receive attention; how I wish I had help,' he continued to roam around the edge of the brook.

After a while, a shell which resembled hard granite covered with green moss appeared before him moving slowly, 'Who goes there, where am I, why are you upset?' Figet asked. 'I need help;

can you please show yourself? I need to talk to you,' hurried Bernard. Figet stopped moving, 'Who are you? Where am I? I am scared,' Figet sounded very scared.

'What! Is this the crazy turtle that is supposed to be powerful!' thought Bernard. 'Why are you scared? I won't eat you obviously, I need your help,' Bernard clearly sounded menacing.

'I don't know, I feel like I am going further deep inside my shell,' Figet sounded almost muted. Bernard realized his mistake, 'Wait! Wait! Wait! I didn't mean to scare you. You are "The Figet", the wisest turtle of all time and only you can help me. You have helped my ancestors and you have superpowers and that sort of thing, you know!' But before he could finish, Figet vanished from the place. Bernard was mad at his failure. He announced that Figet is a myth and if anybody spoke about Figet ever, they will be punished severely.

After several hundred years more, the mystical forest slowly faded out of memory of the civilization which grew around it. There was a kingdom not very far from the forest ruled by a good king. Once the king came to roam the forest with his guard and was lost in a storm. It was told that Figet appeared before the king to save him. That was the last sighting of him in a long time. 'I saw the turtle; it appeared out of nowhere and was reluctant to speak. I had to be very respectful, friendly and kind. When he asked me what I wanted, I requested him to tell its tale and what a fascinating tale it was!' said the dying king to his son. 'If ever you get lost, remember the turtle and may you find the right means to bring him out of his shell to help you,' he said.

As fate would have it, there was treachery in the kingdom and the prince was ousted from the throne by his uncle. He had to flee the country and seek refuge in the dark forest. The guards who chased the prince let go of him when they saw him entering the forest, 'This forest is dark and mysterious; the prince will not last a night in there,' they told each other and left him. The forest indeed was extremely melancholy and dreadful.

The prince was alone and scared. 'My own people turned against me! Father did warn me that wealth and power can corrupt any man! What do I have to live for further?' he told himself. He wandered the forest aimlessly, hoping that some hideous creature would spring from somewhere and kill him. But as the night gave way to day, bright light flooded the forest floor and the prince realized that his eyes were feasting on the most beautiful scenes of his lifetime. The prettiness of the forest exploded as the veil of darkness lifted and he forgot his problems completely in an instant.

'Who goes there?' came a soft voice. The prince thought it was a huge flat boulder covered with green moss moving slowly towards him. 'Here comes the monster finally!' he thought and smiled. 'I am the prince of this kingdom; you can have me whenever you want, creature,' he replied calmly.

'Where am I? Is it a safe place?' spoke the rock. 'You are in the most beautiful place possible. I am sorry, you don't seem to be having the eyes to see. Do you want me to describe it to you what it looks like?' offered the prince with a kind voice.

'Hmm, it has been a while someone showed kindness to me,' said Figet and the prince saw a pair of intense green eyes appear from the hollow of the rock. 'I can see well, I just don't remember who I am and what I am doing here. I might be looking for a friend...,' said Figet looking very lost and looking at the prince suspiciously.

The prince remembered his father's last words. 'Could it be that you are the "great turtle" who helps the needy? Your name is Figet and you have helped my father some time ago,' said the prince. 'I am alone in the forest and who better than you to give me company, I have no friends too,' he said.

Figet wasn't fully convinced for its head still remained concealed. 'Can you walk with me? Are you really harmless and what have you called me? "Figet"? Seems familiar, tell me more, what can I do?' Figet requested. The prince bowed slightly and said, 'My honour! I have heard about you from my father, and he heard it from yourself, here goes your story…,' the prince narrated what he remembered from his father about the turtle.

During the next several days, the prince took care of Figet, narrating his story and ensuring that no harm came to Figet. Finally, after some time, Figet brought his head out completely and regained his full glory. 'O prince! Looks like you have done well to restore my memory; you have given me what it takes to draw me out of my shell; tell me what you seek.'

'Dear friend! I seek nothing but your friendship, as I have told you the day I met you,' the prince replied. 'I see! But you have a need. What is rightfully yours has been taken away from you by treachery. Take this sword and win back your kingdom, but to win back your people fully, you would need the FIGET,' smiled the Turtle as it handed over a dazzling sword to the prince.

'But I have you, don't I have Figet?' asked the Prince. 'Did I not tell your father what Figet truly stands for?' smiled the turtle. 'Listen carefully to what I have to say, for I do not know if you will find me again and if you can draw me out of the shell again….'

The wise turtle spoke, 'Figet of course stands for friendliness, importance (respect), gratitude, environment and trust. One needs to be friendly to deal with my shyness, remind me who I am with respect, show gratitude for what I did, create an environment in which I could open up and gain trust to be able to draw me out completely from my shell and evoke the power that I carried.'

#WorkplaceWhispers

The modern-day workplace is abuzz with interactions. Associates across multiple levels are constantly 'meeting' and exchanging transactions or making decisions (or not!). On most days, a courteous 'how's it going' question to my colleagues or customers results in a 'having too many meetings' response. The relevance and overbearance of meetings (formal or informal) on a working professional cannot be underrated.

While most of these interactions are scripted (and support day-to-day flow of work), some interactions tend to be those where 'connecting with each other' is key for the success of the interaction—inspiring an unwilling colleague that she has the capability to take up that challenging role or resolving a conflict between two individuals/teams or bringing everyone to agree to a key decision or convincing prospect customers that you are trustworthy and they could share their needs/problems with you and so on. And if the individuals coming to these interactions do not open up to each other and remain guarded of their intentions/points of view, then a connect is impossible, and the meetings tend to be laborious, without yielding any result.

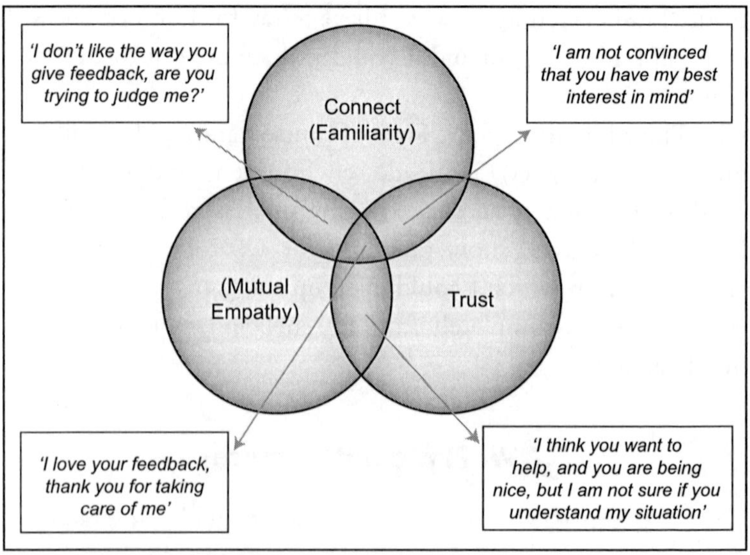

Figure 8.1 The CET Zone

Helping teams understand their latent potential, and constantly nudging them to work towards unlocking it, is both a noble and a daunting endeavour. It requires the leader to have a healthy mix of the ingredients of connect, empathy and trust (CET) with the associate to be able to achieve such a feat (refer to Figure 8.1).

This ability to establish the right CET takes observation and practice. While trust usually tends to be a long-term affair, the other two elements can be practised constantly by turning up regularly towards opportunities, helping a colleague, asking questions, small acts of kindness, appreciation, being more visible, listening keenly and so on. One advice I give to my team is to practise being comfortable with their own voice and develop confidence in speaking, as this is the first step towards making others comfortable.

SEE-ME PROPOSITION? THE FIRST SIGN OF RESPECT

'What is your *see-me proposition* for your customers? Why should they give you time and listen to you? What do we know about their needs or problems which could be included in the see-me proposal?' are common discussion points for those in the sales roles before writing to customers asking for their time. This is not just being empathetic or showing respects towards the individual from whom time was being sought (usually in anticipation of a business opportunity) but also customer centricity in a way (thinking about the prospect even before meeting the person).

I have observed that some of the empathetic senior managers also stick to this practice when it comes to team interactions. Instead of a direct and sometimes cryptic 'I would like to talk to you at this time' or a sudden unannounced call, they take the time to share their 'see-me?' proposition with the associate and explain upfront what they would like to discuss and how this discussion will benefit the associate. This gesture often helps the associate come better prepared and be more oriented to the interaction.

APPROACHING THE GUARDED ONE: REPUTATION AND ENVIRONMENT

Associates tend to be very choosy about who they grant their trust (and to what degree). Unless it is a job interview or a new interaction with no baggage (even here first impressions make an influence on the rest of the conversation), the reputation of the leader and the formality of the environment play a big role in how much an associate will open up and contribute to the conversation. Most associates make up their mind even before the discussion begins as to what they will or will not say.

'Having a friendly disposition at all times and multiple proof points of "meaning well and taking care of the team" are necessary for the leader to gain the trust of the team and get them to participate/share openly. Sometimes discussing in a less overbearing environment also helps,' says Phani Vellanki, a global delivery manager. 'My advice to the team has also been this—If you do not prefer to open up or have to say "No", then let it be so. It is better to say that "I am unwilling to share right now as I am not comfortable," rather than speaking something irrelevant or even worse speaking something incorrect, which might mislead the leader/rest of the team,' he adds.

#Do you recollect such interactions with your team where the associate(s) was unwilling to share? How did you react? Do you put more pressure or try to empathize and connect?

PERSONALITY MR CONSISTENT...

Teams usually find it comfortable for their manager/lead to be consistent in their behaviour—language, tone, medium of communication and so on. Confusing the teams with sudden swings of friendliness and sudden swings of aggression will make them become more guarded and suspicious.

FIGET YOURSELF TOO...

It is also possible that sometimes the associates are not aware of their own potential. Hence, it is important to give perspectives to help them get out of their shell completely, tell them what they are capable of, create an environment of trust and win them over. This is true, maybe more so sometimes when applied to senior people as well. In this case, the elements of mutual trust, importance (what is in it for them/see-me proposition) and gratitude (what they will get in return) will play a role. Figet's character that way is more applicable to a senior executive/ subject matter expert (SME) who probably does not remember you unless you make your mark. And it would take much more than one conversation.

And what most of us may not realize is that FIGET can be applied to ourselves too. For us to be able to break out of the self-imposed shell (mental constraints), we need to talk to ourselves, apply the same FIGET rule and not be too hard on ourselves.

#GameofDrones

AS AN INDIVIDUAL

- I am easily offended and go silent if there is a conflict; I don't share feedback or get into a mode of discussion.
- It is easy to say 'Yes' and nod to everything being spoken rather than engage in a conversation. What if I am misunderstood?

- Even though I am unwilling to speak, when put under pressure I make up something and give incorrect answers.
- I find it hard to say 'No' to my manager.
- I don't have friends at work; I believe that formality is more important.
- I am very self-critical and don't believe that I have something worthwhile to share.
- I think all my teammates are smarter than me; I cannot speak like them.

AS A LEADER

- I want my team to understand me quickly; I hate to repeat myself.
- I do not connect with my team often and one-on-one meetings feel very uncomfortable.
- I don't have a reputation of being approachable.
- I am very persistent in arguments and would like to win with every single point I make.
- I believe that feedback should come only from senior management; team does not know my situation and they are in no position to share feedback.

Now discover and evaluate each roadblock. Think of it as a real drone and see how it is doing. Be honest and review how well you are flying it.

- ☐ **Fully autonomous flight**
- ☐ **Guided flights**
- ☐ **Irregular flight path**
- ☐ **Unwilling to take off**

#KeyResonatingActions

AS AN INDIVIDUAL

- Practise helping others in the team, even in a minor way (supporting with work, organizing events, helping a new joiner and so on).
- Find a friend/mentor with whom you could practise sharing your points of view and taking feedback.
- Find smaller forums to speak, even if for few minutes, and be comfortable listening to your own voice.
- Practise having a (professional) point of view based on data or experience while being open to feedback.
- Ask for connect sessions with your lead/manager regularly to seek and provide feedback.
- If you don't like something at work, share it with at least one individual who can do something about it (or rectify your opinion). This will help in avoiding negative talk or gossip with others who cannot fix the problem.

AS A LEADER

- Work on your reputation. Be kind and approachable while being firm with your views/inputs.
- Express gratitude and appreciation to the team in a timely manner, both when they expect it and when they don't (they didn't think anyone would notice that good thing that they have done silently!).
- Do not give up too fast on your team; persist with making the connect and engaging in conversation.
- Encourage an environment where it is okay to call each other out in a friendly spirit and share feedback.

- Never insult anyone in public, even if they have done something which is not aligned to the expectation.
- Show tolerance to diversity—physical, cognitive, skill-based or others—and not preferential treatment.
- Prefer an easy-to-understand language while communicating; while everyone appreciates a scholar, not many can connect with one.
- Be consistent as much as possible in your responses and not shock the team with sudden mood swings and aggressive outbursts (exceptional circumstances apart).

#StickyNoteWorthy

Silence will save me from being wrong (and foolish), but it will also deprive me of the possibility of being right.

Igor Stravinsky

Reaching beyond the outward shell to truly sense and draw the best from individuals is both a skill and an attribute which one could practise and nurture. Being respectful and friendly should not be confused with shying away from conveying constructive feedback and being tough when necessary. But once the anchor of trust is established, with principles of FIGET at play, even tough (and honest) feedback will be seen as a gesture of affection and genuine concern from the leader and will be well received by the team. This will lead to having truly meaningful and trustworthy conversations in the workplace where individuals do not have to second-guess the intentions behind what is being spoken and a lot of time and resources will be saved.

9

A MATTER OF PRINCIPLE

'Of course, it is a matter of principle!' she said firmly between her sobs. 'You are being very emotional and sentimental, she is just a six-year-old, and clearly they do not understand the difference between right and wrong yet,' said Satish, her husband.

'And that is precisely why the people around these six-year-olds need to act up the right way. I am angry not because our daughter lied to me, but how no one else thinks it is worth the attention. I am not being sentimental; I just care enough not to ignore!' came an angry response.

Both Devi and Satish worked for large multinational corporations and their younger one, Ishita, the six-year-old, was put in an international school close to where they lived. 'I feel we don't give enough time to our children and have delegated the job of bringing them up to teachers and their friends who are constantly bombarding them with their versions of "right",' said Devi.

'I knew it as soon as I saw the marked answer sheet; Ishita is not this dumb; she did fairly well in the previous test which was just last month. No way, she could score so low. When I asked her repeatedly, she kept lying in my face, although very innocently, that it was her answer sheet and she didn't do well this time,' Devi looked enquiringly to ensure Satish was paying attention.

'But after a while she realized that mamma was not happy about this and more importantly that I did not believe her, she came back to me after couple of hours and she was being uncomfortable, so I asked her again this time more gently and lovingly.'

She finally relented and told me the truth. She had exchanged her answer sheets with her friend who got less score and was scared of her mother's scolding.

'They let the first sheet that had their name and roll number be and swapped the other answer sheets. I felt bad when I heard Ishita and I could only blame myself. Is this the moral education that I am/we are giving to our daughter? Is it OK to lie to parents so easily? But what was really horrifying was when I called up Ritu's mom and subsequently Ishita's teacher stating that this is not right, and we should gently tell the kids so. We should talk to them to take out any fears/hesitations which would have made them to act in this way. Imagine my frustration when I received a dismissive response from both. I am sorry for this child Ritu that her mom doesn't think it is important; in fact, she said that it is amusing for her that her daughter thought of something smart like this! And the teacher! I asked the teacher that she should speak to the children and may be redo the test to set an example to both, and she did not think it was worth the trouble! Can you believe this?' Devi narrated the event third time in the evening, although she was being much crisper the third time around.

'It may seem silly to overreact to these things, Satish, but don't you see that kids of today will grow up working in companies like ours and are made responsible for big decisions later in life. How can they be entrusted with fair dealings when their foundation is so shaky? I mean, is it not common these days that associates fake the mandatory tests just to get the job done, or do not find it difficult at all to lie on your face? At least I can see right through the person when they are lying to me and I tell them that it is OK to be honest and it is good in the long run. Getting favours and fake appreciation seems to be the way forward, especially around certain times of the year! I feel for them and I wish I could do something more…,' she said.

'I think it is especially important to bring them up "right" in the initial days of their career and lay a strong foundation. Else there is an easy pitfall of "just get it done, doesn't matter how",' she added. 'Are you referring to your team not following coding standards again?' enquired Satish with a wink. 'That and many other things! Having objections to what you are told to do is OK, but not openly talking about it and trying to find shortcuts is the issue,' came a firm reply.

As they discussed late into the night, Devi recollected a story from her childhood. 'I was a good student, but there was this instance when I could not solve a math problem. I didn't want to let my teacher down and decided to lie to her.' Devi narrated the following incident.

> 'Ma'am, yesterday evening I was helping my mother with cooking and accidentally I cut my index finger as I was peeling carrots,' little Devi said, showing her hand with the finger wrapped in band-aid. 'Oh dear! Was it painful? You should be more careful na; don't worry about homework, I am sure you understand the topic, please take your seat,' the teacher responded benevolently. She thought she could get by the moment easily and buy some more time to work on the problem, but the thought of cheating her teacher was even more difficult to handle than the embarrassment of failing at the problem.
>
> That was the last period of the day, and as the children started walking out of the class, the teacher called out to her. 'I have an easy way to cure cuts from peeling carrots. Come sit with me, dear,' she said. And she took the next 20 minutes explaining the math problem

and practical applications of it. 'If you imagine it this way, it is very easy to understand geometry; look at the shape of that building for instance…,' she continued and helped her understand the problem.

'I get it, ma'am; I can solve it now,' Devi's eyes moistened.

'Now shall we see if the wound is healed, dear?' she said with a smile. 'I am sorry, ma'am. I will never do this again, but how did you know…?' she said between sniffing and sobbing.

'You will know dear when you gain some experience as you grow. When you lie you will not be yourself; for instance, you were not looking at me, your shoulders were drooped and you just wanted to run away. Then I saw you sit in your place as if someone placed hundred heavy geometrical shapes on your head,' she laughed.

'That is a great incident, and now I know what gives you strength to be honest…,' said Satish, 'Incidents early in life where someone showed you the "right" thing to do with kindness and empathy, wish we all had such teachers throughout our life!'

'I think we do if we look for them and encourage honesty in each other. It is a matter of principle and practice. You cannot be casual all the time and expect guidance from outside. And of course when someone does take the initiative to be forthright—makes a mistake for instance and comes forth boldly talking about it—he/she should not be thrown under the bus, rather made an example to others and should receive help. I say this to my team all the time. Be honest and bring out the problems early. While sometimes it is frustrating to rectify issues brought to one's attention (especially when not done in a timely manner), and sometimes people do not seem to react the right way, eventually they will like you for your honesty. The world is desperately looking for people who could be trusted, more than anything else. Skills will come along the way…,' she concluded philosophically as Satish struggled to stifle his yawns.*

#WorkplaceWhispers

CARE ENOUGH NOT TO IGNORE

Real work gets done by those who 'care enough not to ignore'. And good news is that every individual displays this attribute, to a certain degree. Remember the days when you stayed up all night to work on a production issue or to help a struggling colleague or to ensure that a report is prepared in time for the executive meeting the next day or took time out from your busy schedule to mentor someone from your team? All these and more such instances displayed by empathetic individuals like you, hold the workplace together day after day. Even a minor slip during these times when the workplace needs your 'care' could be devastating and cause serious damage to the reputation of the organization or potential revenue loss.

And this, let's call it 'professional sensitivity', is the top attribute that managers and customers look for when they interview candidates, especially in project management or leadership roles. Consider the following hypothetical situation.

Iqbal is an onshore delivery manager working for a large multinational customer, responsible for operations. As Iqbal is about to close the day and hit bed, he gets an SMS alert suggesting that one of the critical applications has crossed an operational threshold. If the teams do not act on it immediately, it might result in severe problems, resulting in millions of dollars loss in revenue for the customer. It is 11.30 PM *in his time zone*

* The above story is inspired by real incidents in the family of a couple working in large organizations.

and early hours for the offshore and near-shore teams. In 10 minutes he gets another alert suggesting that no one has acted on the problem. He needs to act now and bring together a SWAT team of decision-makers from customer organization, his team and potentially the vendor team in the next 30 minutes.

When such a crisis hits, it is not the industry expertise or skills on the resume that come to the rescue. It is the moral courage backed by a genuine 'care' for resolving the situation and preventing the impending crisis. And customers deeply care for individuals with such attributes. If you have such individuals in your team, you are lucky and I am sure you are giving them the gift of your time constantly, if not anything more.

HONESTY IS THE ONLY STRATEGY

I recollect several interactions with customers across different geographies and cultures where they said something in the lines of 'I understand that people err, mistakes happen, and as leaders we need to do our best to help them rectify those and put the right processes in place. All this can be done, but if we remain transparent and work with honesty. As long as we remain honest with each other, we can have a great relationship....' This is not just applicable to ways of working with customers but also with teams in an organization. Teams tend to appreciate and even empathize with the constraints of leadership as long as there is transparency and honesty.

#GameofDrones

AS AN INDIVIDUAL

- There are several aspects at my workplace which I do not appreciate, but I keep them to myself and not share feedback.

- When I notice potential problems in a project or when I make a mistake, I hesitate in taking it to my project leader.
- I seldom appreciate my colleagues or my manager when I notice a good behaviour exhibited by them.
- Nothing but monetary appreciation excites me.
- I think it is okay to be casual at work once in a while; everyone around me seems to be so.
- It is okay to miss deadlines, as long as there is a good excuse.

AS A LEADER

- I have zero tolerance for mistakes of the team, and they know this.
- I prefer rules and metrics to control the team; there is no time for inspiration or motivation.
- I tend to appreciate outcomes only, that's what we get paid for and not behaviours. As long as the outcome is there, I don't bother about how it is being achieved.
- I find it hard to replicate success, because we don't usually understand why we succeeded.

Now discover and evaluate each roadblock. Think of it as a real drone and see how it is doing. Be honest and review how well you are flying it.

☐ **Fully autonomous flight**

☐ **Guided flights**

☐ **Irregular flight path**

☐ **Unwilling to take off**

#KeyResonatingActions

- Allocate a section of time in team meetings to discuss good things at work, even if they are minor.
- Be sensitive to and show interest in receiving feedback from a colleague or team member.
- Encourage the team to be bold about sharing 'what is broken' quickly (instead of sitting on it).
- Be bold in bringing up your points of view to your leads or managers.
- Meet often to discuss the undesirable practices which have been observed, in a spirit of kindness and empathy, and alert everyone to be watchful.
- Reward employees with a high say/do ratio (champions of integrity); make them as examples for others.
- After every success, get together to 'understand the success and how it came to be' more than celebrate the success.

#StickyNoteWorthy

You will find ultimately every great man is a principle and not a person.

- Dr K. C. Varadachari

While good teams are a showcase of high skills and competence of individuals, *great teams are a showcase of principles and values in action* from highly engaged individuals working together as a unit. The formative years of every employee are most precious and the environment that they get exposed to during this time would have an enormous influence on how they will drive the organization as they grow. It is easier to practise a principle (integrity, honesty) if the entire team culture is attuned to it.

Similar to the slogan we commonly hear while dealing with aspects of security that says 'Security is everyone's responsibility,' the attribute of 'caring enough' as a team to 'not ignore' should be everyone's active outlook. And leadership has a key role to play in building the needed boldness in the teams to step up and perform at the highest levels of ethos possible.

10

THREE QUESTIONS

Legend has it that in an ancient kingdom called Prajnapura, the king suddenly developed a rare disease and was heading towards a slow and painful death. The court physician tried all medicines of the land and finally announced, 'Only the miraculous flower of Chakra that grows on the mountain top of Sadhanagiri can cure him.' But everyone knew that conquering that mountain was impossible. *There was no evidence of anyone even attempting the climb* through the treacherous forests and some of the deadliest creatures living undisturbed. Prajnapura had a valiant prince in Manav who had just finished his education and returned to the palace.

'Is it true that no one can make it to the top?' Manav enquired his teacher. But before his teacher could respond, 'No one who did claims it, and no one in their sane mind would attempt such a feat', replied the chief minister.

'That is true; we do not have proof; no one claimed it. But it is not true that no one conquered it. In fact, I had a chance encounter with a brilliant looking man once who mentioned that "conquering Sadhanagiri was not his biggest achievement in life…,"' the teacher replied.

'But what does it mean, master, he has climbed the mountain? If I find him, can he help me get to the top?' asked Manav.

'Not him, he was just a disciple; you need to find the one who can teach you to climb and chart the safest path to the top. *Your real quest is not climbing the mountain, it is finding the one that can help you get there!*' said the teacher.

'Indeed! There are several villages scattered all across the base, and several less-known dwellers—hermits, village folk and tribal people. Can I do this, master?' exclaimed the prince. 'I have taught you well, Manav; use your learning appropriately; all you need is three questions to solve the problem, and choosing wisely on who you would ask which question,' the teacher smiled. 'Please tell me what they are, master,' Manav bowed as he waited for a response from his teacher.

'The first question is: ***What is your goal?*** *What are you living for? What is your purpose?* The way you ask may depend on who you are asking. The second question is: ***What do you practise?*** *What is your method? How are you moving forward?* And the third question is: ***Who is your master?*** *Who is your teacher? Who is your guide or what is guiding you?*' said the teacher.

'I don't understand, master! Where do I start! Who do I ask?' asked Manav. 'Obviously, the people you seek are the ones with a goal of climbing. So you cannot start with those who are far away from the mountain or those in the valley villages. *You will have to make at least the initial climb* to meet those who have made their living slightly above the base,' the teacher smiled.

Manav started his quest with blessings from his teacher. As he made the climb of this huge mountain, he found several small dwellings on the slopes. Most of these dwellers had one thing in common—they knew how to climb to some degree.

'Why have you chosen to stay so far away from the base and on the mountain slopes?' Manav asked.

'The resources here are plentiful; we have everything that we need and collectively we make the rest, but they say that *as you go up, the bounty gets better and better*, some extraordinary forests and exquisite waterfalls, some say even the fountain of life might be up there somewhere,' the dwellers said.

'What is your goal?' Manav asked naively.

'What!? We told you, to be here, happily, no more climbing,' they said. 'But you know how to climb well; you have come this far; can you teach me how you practised climbing? Who taught you?' he asked. 'Some of us were born here, but there are few elders who made the climb a long time ago; they might help.' So Manav learnt a few lessons from the elders of this community and climbed on further.

He met several dwellings on his way up, and in some of the dwellings he found that the people were either without a goal or without the right methods or the right guide. And he found a connection too. *Those who did not have a goal usually did not remember any methods too.* 'If you do not practise and pass it on to your next generation, how will you remember any methods?' he told himself, 'And you will not remember who taught you to get here in the first place.' *He swiftly moved on from such dwellings* and took a circular route in view of finding the next dwelling which might help him take the next level on the mountain.

After much persistent efforts, he finally started to find dwellings where he saw that the dwellers had one aim in their life, 'To move their dwelling to the next level of the mountain and give a better life to their progeny', they said. 'Not that we are not happy here, but our life's fulfilment comes from taking on this mountain, and the mountain pays us back with so much bounty. If we don't succeed, our children at least will, we know there are dwellers further up, assisted by able teachers,' their words encouraged Manav. He learnt their methods quickly and moved on and eventually succeeded with his quest. He found the teacher that would teach him how to climb and what path to take to make it to the top safely and get to the Chakra flower.

The inspiration for this story comes from working with some very talented associates who have figured out the art of learning.

Each one of us have (professional) aspirations to look forward to—some translate into measurable goals, while some remain tacitly inside acting as little inner voices qualifying the day-to-day work that we do. And when we meet someone at workplace who seems to be displaying the attributes that we would want to see in ourselves, there is a natural sense of appreciation for them: 'Ah! Here is how I would like to talk...' or 'Here is how I would like to approach a problem' or 'Here is how I want to make a presentation' and so on. And unlike some of the others who stop here with a silent appreciation, some of us tend to take a step further and build a mentoring relationship with such individuals.

THE IMPORTANT KYC: KNOW YOUR 'COLLEAGUES'

When you join a new team (or a company), it is natural to get an induction on the customer (or the other groups that you will serve) and the organization (as part of the KYC initiative—know your customer/know your company). The third and equally important aspect of KYC which doesn't get due attention is getting to *know your colleagues*. Some of this discovery may happen over a course of time during a project or other informal interactions, but it is important to maintain a sense of interest in the company (team around) that you are part of with an intent to discover their strengths, skills and practices and eventually learn from them.

UNSTATED UNLESS THERE IS A RESIGNATION OR A NEW YEAR PARTY

It has been an interesting experience being an audience to some of the 'farewell meet-ups' to associates leaving the organization. Several good things are spoken naturally, but more importantly, the detail that is brought out in sharing 'how exactly the associate that is leaving has helped during times of great need, what specific skills and attributes he/she has displayed to support the team…' and so on by some of the individuals in the meeting is very heartening to hear. But what is not so good to hear is when the associate leaving responds with 'Wow! You never told me that you appreciated that … very glad to hear now.'

Similar interactions are noted during New Year meet-ups or some big programme milestones where associates are significantly 'moved' by the atmosphere and come out to shower 'intricate and specific' appreciation on the others. Appreciation need not be such a sparse spectacle! And this is also the first step in getting someone to help you or mentor you with a skill/attribute that you would like to learn yourself. Telling them 'in as much honesty and detail' that you can muster as to *what about* and *how much* you appreciate their skill not only helps them find motivation for themselves but also opens them up to help you.

#Can you reflect on the pattern of your appreciation to others in your team?

INDULGING IN RIGHT QUESTIONS AND GETTING TO PRACTISE

Once a connect has been made via sincere appreciation, the pace of learning depends upon the quality of questions (the three questions being part of them) and working to a personal plan. It is not uncommon to hear associates saying, 'What you do is amazing, getting up so early every day to read and practise, woah! I can never do that, not my cup of tea....' Learning about the goals and good practices of mentors would amount to nothing if they are not actually put to practise, and although this is the hardest bit, this is where the rubber would actually hit the road.

#GameofDrones

- I do not work with personal goals (short or long term) and just keep to the work assigned.
- I am not aware of any SMEs at my workplace; I am not sure how to look for them.
- I am focused only on getting the next opportunity, do things to please my seniors/manager and gain visibility.
- I have several experts in the team in various areas, but I have not taken the initiative to approach them for mentoring.
- We have a great time as a team and deliver good stuff together, but my skills/learning have not improved in a long time.
- I am very sensitive to feedback (I don't receive it very well!), and this might be keeping the seniors in the team from taking the initiative to coach me more proactively.
- I shower a lot of praise on the good performers, some of whom are my good friends at work, but don't ask them for any help to learn their skills.
- As a manager, I keep my good resources always busy; they should be focused on delivering stuff and not in teaching others, this is not a school.
- As a senior associate, some call me an SME. I spend all my time in working or learning more myself. I have not mentored others. I don't have good associates in the team at a level that I can mentor.

Now discover and evaluate each roadblock. Think of it as a real drone and see how it is doing. Be honest and review how well you are flying it.

- ☐ **Fully autonomous flight**
- ☐ **Guided flights**
- ☐ **Irregular flight path**
- ☐ **Unwilling to take off**

#KeyResonatingActions

- Start with a self-evaluation in an area of interest where you would like to improve—this will help establish a personal baseline.
- Look for individuals within your team or organization in this area of your interest who you appreciate and can learn from.
- Be specific and elaborate while sharing appreciation. This tends to make it more genuine and helps in connecting with the individuals better.
- Persist while asking for help. Share your efforts in learning (the subject) with the mentor and ask specific questions on where and how you need help.
- Thank the mentor openly in forums and share the impact of this mentoring with management.
- As a senior associate (or an expert), be willing to train others by sharing your best practices and helping others set up the right goals.
- As a manager, constantly identify associates with good skills as well as attributes and map them with others that they can groom.

- Provide visibility to these associates within the team and across teams and encourage them to practise mentoring as one of the key activities.

#StickyNoteWorty

Even five minute meaningful conversations with other people not only fuel us in the moment but also build up a reserve of social capital so that when hard times strike, we can draw down on that bank account.

Michelle Gielan

The potential of a workplace/organization goes beyond the direct line of work and the monetary benefits it provides. There is so much to learn from each other by engaging in the right conversations, appreciating/nurturing the good attributes in the team and continuously aspiring towards higher goals.

11 THE FOUNDATION

Once upon a time, there was a unique village called Dhanyapuram. The people of the village were the kindest of souls and lived as one big family. Those who visited the village for trade or for their rich vegetable markets felt extremely well taken care of. The hospitality was out of the world, and the dealings were kind. It is said that no one could ever trick the people of this village, as they were protected by their collective good.

'Something is really weird about them,' said a cloth trader from a neighbouring village to another merchant on their way back from Dhanyapuram. 'They spend a lot of time enquiring about our goods, who have helped make them, and they offered their thanks to each and every one. I thought at first that this was one eccentric person with a lot of time at his hand, but then every other customer who visited me to buy clothes did the same. They were not willing to buy unless I told them all about how we make the clothes, and who is involved. And they did not bargain for money, paid duly what I charged them,' he added. 'I have similar experience, looks like they are simpletons,' remarked another.

Now there was a third merchant who was visiting Dhanyapuram for quite some time in his life. 'Simpletons? Far from it. It is their belief system that makes them behave so. They believe that if "one is not thankful for what they receive, the value of what is received vanishes sooner or later". They practise thankfulness as a way of life in that village. Do you know why no one can cheat them? Because they are so truthful themselves,' he said.

'What rubbish! I will prove you wrong; let us make a visit tomorrow again and test this out,' challenged the first merchant who was called Somu. The three of them decided to make another trip to Dhanyapuram the next day.

Somu, the cloth merchant, Dina, the elder merchant, and Anand, the third merchant, visited Dhanyapuram and went to a small tiffin centre. 'I know the old lady who runs this place; she serves great local food,' said Dina as he wished the old woman who received them as if they were her close relatives. 'Don't they get bored with this *ever-humble act*?' Somu retorted. 'Be gentle; she is not acting; she is a kind person,' said Dina.

They were served with local tiffin and other delicacies which they ate to their heart's content. Dina requested the server to call for the old lady and when she arrived, he thanked her, the chef and the server for their kind treatment and tasty food. 'This will sustain us for the day, amma, God bless you,' he said and looked at the other two expecting them to follow along. Somu and Anand simply said, 'Ya, it's good. We might come back soon.' The old lady said, 'We will be very happy to serve you again, son.'

As soon as they stepped out of the centre, Somu felt extremely light in the stomach as if he had not eaten in days. 'I feel the same too, can't believe we ate three persons' fill just a few minutes ago,' said Anand. 'Three persons' fill? I ate more like three oxen fill, but I can't move an inch without some food now,' cried Somu looking at Dina. 'I told you before, this is a place where "thankfulness is a living trait"; if you don't follow along, *what you receive thanklessly will lose its effect instantly*. Rush inside before it's too late and thank the old lady and her staff heartfully, and if I might add with a sense of remorse,' advised Dina. Somu and Anand rushed back inside immediately to the old lady.

Through the rest of the day, Dina took the other two merchants around and explained to them the uniqueness of Dhanyapuram and its inhabitants. 'They come together every week to thank their farmers and other craftsmen and understand if the village people can collectively help someone in need,' he said. 'When I visited this place for the first time, I wanted to cheat these "simpletons", by selling them poor-quality material and buying all I want from their produce. But as soon as I left the village boundaries, all that I bought turned to dust and I had to immediately rectify my mistake,' he recollected.

'This appears too good to be true. Are there no others from the village who are thankless and unmindful? I mean *that is natural for the rest of us outside Dhanyapuram, isn't it? I do not remember saying "thank you" to my mother in a long time, and she doesn't seem to mind. Ya, I thank outside folk for formality, you got to do what you got to do for business, right…?'* Somu spoke honestly. 'I am glad that the place is already having its effect on you, you are being very truthful,' Dina smiled. 'Yes, there are a few who do not practise it naturally; in fact, you are in luck; see that young man approaching us? What do you make of him?' asked Dina pointing at a pale-looking young man.

'He is moving like he is carrying a ton of weight on his shoulders, although he is not carrying anything. Why does he look like he hasn't taken a bath in a while? Haven't seen someone look so dull and dark since morning,' remarked Anand.

'They call it "*the weight of thanklessness* around here,"' said Dina. 'But the villagers don't give up on such people. They see *thanklessness as a disease*, and people who happen to exhibit it get special attention and even more support. The best way to deal with thankless people is by *being kind* to them and *repeatedly reminding them of the support they have*,' he added.

'From what we have seen so far, such people may not have the means to live on their own very long here…,' reflected Somu. 'Right you are, brother; I am glad you have understood the power of this place; let us return now,' said Dina as he alighted the bullock cart.

#WorkplaceWhispers

A natural corollary to the aspect of 'finding one's place'—'giving due credit to the contributions' of others—is an important attribute of a fulfilling workplace. There is a great joy in knowing that you have made someone successful with your work/support—a manager, an onshore technician, a customer and so on. And it is even more joyful if there is an honest acknowledgement of the same. If one pauses to look keenly, there is a high degree of interdependence in a modern workplace which is increasingly getting complex. There are layers and layers of multi-tier teams delivering to each other before an end customer is impacted.

And it is ever more important to be mindful of contributions from all around which are helping us keep up to our promises and stay relevant.

'THE TEAM BEHIND...'

'Especially those of us in the frontline roles, acting as the face of the larger team, should ensure that we represent them well and give them the needed visibility. We should share detailed feedback from the customers but also every bit of appreciation that we get day in day out' was a common message from the leadership teams that I have worked with across multiple programmes. I also had the joy to work with several customers who, after every successful project milestone, insist to be connected to the entire team and pass on their appreciation in person (or over a videoconference call). And as a customer, having a keen sense of appreciation for your suppliers would help you foment good relationships or end up losing them otherwise.

Being thankful to the others is one thing, but having a thankful attitude is even more powerful.

GRATITUDE LEADING TO EXCELLENCE

'I started my career in the engineering industry, doing material management, where I learnt the elements of both gratitude and sincerity. I think the latter comes from the former—sincerity is a natural by-product of being grateful and thankful. After about 18 years, I hit a plateau and had to move to Enterprise Resource Planning (software). And again after few years, I had to move into yet another area which required more learning. In all of these different roles that I performed, maintaining a sense of gratitude helped me to be honest with everyone and sincere with myself. Both these attributes helped me gain one project after another. Customers and managers love honesty and entrust more responsibilities. Being sincere is not just a good-to-have attribute for me, but it also has been a great enabler. I owe all the progress I have made in my professional career to the 30 minutes head start I have had every single day in the past 35 years of my career, as an example,' says Milind Vad, an analytics platforms expert and an accomplished engagement manager, who is few months away from 'declaring his innings' (professional retirement described in his own words).

THE BIG PICTURE VIEW

Being thankful and appreciative also requires one to be contextually aware of the opportunity and the associated impact. Sometimes working in back office or support groups makes it difficult to understand the end customer impact and if there is any relevance to the monotonous work being done. Here is where the role of senior associates or leadership in the team should come in to connect the day-to-day actions with real-world impact. How creating a good design or doing a good job with QA is getting translated into *connecting people reliably (telecommunications) or helping the world transact safely (banking) or helping factory worker safety (manufacturing) or ensuring power plants run in an uninterrupted manner (utilities) and so on.* This big picture connect provides purpose to the team and helps them better appreciate their own efforts and invest themselves more meaningfully. But is it possible or practical to connect every single activity in a workplace to an end customer influence? Maybe not so, at least directly, but there is always a beneficiary, and knowing whose life we are making a difference to (and in what ways) always helps.

THOSE WHO NEVER GET A 'THANK YOU'

There are some individuals or groups who are always in the firing line. They don't get appreciated when they do their job but get into the firing line when they miss out on something, even a minor thing. Do you see such groups or individuals around you? Time to stop by and say a 'thank you'?

The CIO Mitchell Whitman was visiting the offshore development centre of his partner organization. Towards the end of the day, an award ceremony was organized to appreciate the individuals and teams that had provided exemplary support throughout the year. Several awards were given to the teams—'Solving highest number of problems in an area', 'Most complex problem resolved in a business application', 'Walking the extra mile in resolving incidents' and so on. After the awards were given, Mitchell asked for one specific team and was taken to their work zone. 'We have given awards to the other teams for resolving the problems quickly or working hard to fix difficult problems. No doubt, they deserve praise. But this team here, they have done something even more wonderful. They have ensured that ***no problems have come up in the first place*** *for the entire year and more. They have worked so silently* *that we may tend to forget them. They deserve highest praise, and here is my special award for them,' he concluded.*

Here's to all the support groups, personal assistants, ops teams and all those who work behind the scenes silently—THANK YOU!

#GameofDrones

- I am not aware of or appreciative of the support I get from my extended team.
- I hardly ever pass on the appreciation I receive to someone else; most of the time I am the reason and drive for my success.
- I don't mind taking credit for the work done by others in the team; if I am representing the work, I deserve to get the visibility.
- I am usually resentful of my work situation and engage in gossip with others to make them also feel so.
- I don't feel contented with what has been achieved; the focus is always on the next big milestone to hit.
- We don't ever give credit to the support teams; they are not directly involved in delivering to the customer anyway.
- I tend to be extremely resentful if I don't get appreciated for my work.
- I see so many thankless people in my workplace, but I have not given any feedback to them or to my manager.
- As a manager, I have a reporting hierarchy; I interact with my first-line subordinates only and pass on all the appreciation for success to them or penalize them for failures.

Now discover and evaluate each roadblock. Think of it as a real drone and see how it is doing. Be honest and review how well you are flying it.

- ☐ **Fully autonomous flight**
- ☐ **Guided flights**
- ☐ **Irregular flight path**
- ☐ **Unwilling to take off**

#KeyResonatingActions

- Try to understand the support structure in place at your workplace—all those frameworks and individuals that are helping you to perform every day.
- Practise appreciation—find opportunities to share appreciation to the individuals, especially if they are remote (either by location or by structure).
    - o Find a mentor/friend in the team who can help you practise this art.
- Discourage gossip and try to interact with individuals instead of spreading assumptions.
- Share visibility and success.
- Be kind to those who seem to be taking you for granted, but provide persistent feedback.
- As a manager, constantly share the big picture and elevate the work done by the team.

#StickyNoteWorthy

If I have seen further than others, it is by standing upon the shoulders of giants.

Isaac Newton

There is a lot of research and material behind the 'science of gratitude' in promoting physical and emotion well-being of individuals. Organizations are constantly striving to codify this in their processes. Despite best efforts, omissions tend to happen, and sometimes people tend to get missed out and left out. Instead of being resentful during those times, treating the omissions with kindness and sharing timely feedback will be helpful. Developing a culture of appreciation and ensuring that every contributing hand gets its due share of credit provide a solid foundation for the team to stand on and makes the workplace a joyful one.

12 SPEAKING RESPECTFULLY

'Your stories and morals may not have practical application, granny,' Hari took a deep breath.

'Why! Something happened at work today, Hari?' smiled the grandma.

'Well, sometimes I feel that *speaking out is being taken as disrespect* … and a few from my team also tell me that they don't want to get into conflict, so they keep quiet…,' Hari spoke quickly, as if he was afraid that someone from his team will listen to this complaint.

Grandma gave a broad smile, 'I also told you that your generation tends to misinterpret the reactions and reach conclusions too soon. *You should not give up on each other so soon. If you do an activity with sincerity and with no mal-intent, people will get it eventually.* Even if the activity is speaking up and speaking out what you think, do it often, and make people understand that that's who you are by nature, instead of getting bottled up and not sharing what you think is right. *It may be so that sometimes, what you think is right, may not be so.* And then if someone counters you and proves that your understanding is wrong, you *should be open to accept it.* Focus should be on the task at hand and *not on what someone is thinking about you….*'

'Hmm … I guess it needs some getting used to. My previous team was different, and now this is a new group, and here I think people are slightly weird … anyway…,' Hari paused again.

To bring some perspective and help Hari out, his granny narrated a story her grandfather told her.

My grandfather was a sarpanch (head of a few villages grouped together in that precinct) and was highly regarded and loved by the people even from the surrounding villages. He encouraged open discussions and promoted self-governance as much as practically possible. He used to say to my father, 'Always give your people freedom to speak in front of you. Never judge or crucify them for challenging your judgement; spend time to convince and encourage discussion. Allowing people to contribute and share is a very good way to make them feel connected with the larger problem, and even if the problems are not always solved, it will give them a sense of accomplishment, for having been heard, and attempting the solutions.'

There was a dispute on the boundaries of the agricultural lands that overlapped with another region, and how the water supply from the river should be handled. A meeting was called to go through the facts and settle this and the sarpanch of the other village came to my grandfather's village along with a large group of his people. They agreed to meet at the square, hear out each other's arguments and take a fair decision agreeable to both the parties.

I recollect the name of the other sarpanch was Sankarappa, and he was a well-respected but also most-feared sarpanch in his region. 'Who will speak from your side, Ramaiah?' he demanded my grandfather. 'What, is that so important? Okay, I will ask Raju to present our side of the facts,' he said. 'Is he your son? Son-in-law? Can he talk well? I will be the one taking up our case,' Sankarappa looked at his village elders and spoke in a rude tone.

'He is the farmer who is *most impacted by our dispute* and understands the problem and also the facts around the matter; we will all support him and you as well if we get to the understanding that you are correct, and we have misunderstood the situation to start with,' replied my grandfather, 'Let me narrate our understanding first and I will ask Raju to share his concerns with us all,' he added.

'Very well, Ramaiah; we shall see; I was expecting this to be a discussion between two sarpanchs in power; have not come all the way to speak to a farmer,' Sankarappa showed his frustration.

As Ramaiah, my grandfather, tried to describe the boundaries of the lands and the consumption of the river water, Raju and some other farmers cut in between to add a few minor details and then described in detail on how the water should be diverted, and how this will benefit Sankarappa's village as well. 'In my village, we don't speak out of turn; don't disrespect your sarpanch by speaking out of turn,' he yelled at Raju and others.

'Sir, in our village it is quite common to speak freely. By speaking up, we didn't disrespect our sarpanch; in fact, we will never disrespect him even if we have to lose our lives; we just did what he always encouraged us to do,' said Somu, another farmer.

As the group broke for a late lunch organized by my grandfather, our village folk took utmost care of everyone from Sankarappa's village and ensured that they were properly fed before they took their own lunch.

'First you humiliate us and then you enact so much care and concern, what is this ploy?' Sankarappa questioned my grandfather.

'We were respecting you when we challenged you, and we are respecting you when we are serving you, sir,' said Raju, 'We are taught by our sarpanch that *if we don't tell the truth, and support the opinion of the leader for fear or favour, that is real disrespect.* Here in our village we do not put boundaries on who should be respected; *we respect everyone, even* the *disabled. But when it comes to challenging what is not right, we do not hold back.* It is not a sign of disrespect,' he added.

By the end of that day, Sankarappa and his village elders not only agreed to the facts presented by Raju and other farmers but also understood that by encouraging everyone to participate in the problem, my grandfather prepared all of them to understand the problem, explore the facts thoroughly and present what was right for both the parties. 'I fell in love with your governance, dear sir. I would like you to coach me and my elders to learn your ways of dealing with village affairs. I heard some stories of your village and your ways, but this dispute has given me first-hand experience,' Sankarappa said before he took leave.

'And what if I end up with a set-up which is not willing to listen?' Hari asked as the story finished.

'Ugh! Jumping to conclusions again! You should *fundamentally believe that people are good, all of them.* No one wilfully tries to carry malicious intent and subdue others. It is possible that sometimes they are misguided, entertain the thoughts of illusion of control over everything and feel insecure if others do not obey. *But keep making sincere attempts, to understand and be understood, it works.... If it is not working, try harder; don't give up easy, else you will miss your learning.*'

'I wish we had more people like your grandfather, don't you think granny?'

'Why do you think they are not there? Look hard enough and you will find them, and you also strive to be an enabling person in your team, as you grow up, and ... now...,' she looked intently.

#WorkplaceWhispers

Given a chance, I am sure all of us would want to be in a team where individuals can express without fear of being judged or frowned upon. Even better if we get a mentor who can constantly help us with the art of 'making a point', which is a key skill to practise and improve all through one's career.

TWO ELEMENTS OF 'THE PITCH'

The first element is the speaking manners of the place and being sensitive to your audience's 'listening conventions' (the language used in the place, the terminology of the place/domain, Dos and Don'ts, when to speak/stop talking and so on). As they say, 'Communication is not what is spoken, but what is understood.' The second element is having the courage to receive feedback and stand corrected. This openness will declutter the mind and help to make a confident pitch in the first place, without hesitation.

BEING PART OF THE DECISION-MAKING: A SIGN OF TRUST

'Once you have identified "your team", meaning you know that they have the mettle to walk along with you, it is important that they are invited to the table to make their voices heard. This is particularly important while facing a complex decision point. Of course, the leader should have the ability to control the discussion and drive conviction in the team all along. Then we will execute the decision together,' says Håkan Sessle, a technology leader and SME, responsible for implementing and running complex cloud systems. 'Allowing the team to participate will also make them prepare and put their skin in the game. And as a programme driver, I get to learn what they are thinking, that is very important,' he adds.

BEING RIGHT, WITHOUT BEING HARSH

In a company which dealt with developing supply and logistics software, several years ago there was once a complex programme which involved teams from multiple geographies to deliver a product. The delivery of this software product meant a big deal for the company. At a time when the product was nearing the date of release, the QA team responsible for clearing the final software package hit a tough decision point. They had to reject the build sent by the development team which belonged to a different geography. It was a tough decision, and rejecting this build meant that the overall programme milestones would be pushed by several months. There was an escalation meeting called by the head of development challenging this decision.

Chandrasekhar Solasa, an accomplished programme leader of the organization, was responsible for the overall delivery to the customer. He let the QA lead to drive the discussion while he was in the room monitoring the conversation. The discussion started off on an aggressive note and was getting to become rude. The QA team was getting bulldozed for the rejection and was being pushed to the corner. The lead could not take it any longer and was about to retaliate strongly when Chandra hit the mute button on the phone and said, 'Tone it down, guys, make your point without hurting the other side; that you are right doesn't mean you have to be harsh. It is natural that they are upset, we rejected their work. We will win them over by being kind but firm.' The QA team persisted with a kind tone. They managed to explain to the other team on the merits of the rejection and how they could support them deliver a better version of the package next time. This leadership intervention at the right time changed how the teams worked with each other, and together they succeeded in releasing the product to market with a few months of delay.

CONVICTION AND PARTICIPATION OF THE TEAM ARE KEYS TO SUCCESS

While there is no doubt that leadership has a crucial role in instilling the right character in the team, conviction of the team in adopting those characters is equally important. One of the key reasons for failure of several important programmes is lack of conviction in the team driving these programmes and inability to come together as one unit.

Here is a narrative from Marie-Josee Leblond, a senior executive from the industry, on a programme which we executed together.

I remember once leading one of these large 'never-done-before' modernization programmes on a hypercomplex central legacy system with multiple stakeholders. The modernization had been attempted many times in the past by others but to no avail. On the onset, we faced massive resistance of the type 'tried before—can't be done'. Except for four of us in a room, no one else believed it could be done. We realized early that to succeed, we had to set the right change strategy to *convince* all that this can be done. We started by making sure that all stakeholders understood the urgency of the situation and found a common starting point. We then set and anchored visionary goals. From there, we worked on small achievable increments to build momentum towards achieving the larger goals. The first phase was executed in a year and was recognized as a tremendous success. We had a competent and courageous team, no doubt, but the key differentiating success factor was our ability to keep all stakeholders engaged throughout the programme. Losing even one stakeholder could have jeopardized the whole programme.

'Complex programmes tend to be so not just because of the technical complexity that needs to be dealt with but also the number of stakeholders involved who have a say in the programme. In my experience, successfully driving such programmes requires that the programme manager and team are able to drive "continuous conviction" with the stakeholders by being bold and honest, but also showing progress, succeeding in small milestones, nudging everyone to take decisions and constantly showing the big picture. We should always strive to bring people together without judging them,' says Lakshay Dhir, an accomplished programme and engagement manager from a large organization.

BEING OPEN TO LEARNING FROM THE TEAM

'I always tell my colleagues, junior or senior, that they should believe in themselves, always try to emulate the good from others and have a high benchmark for their work. I tell them that "I am no different than you and I achieve results by dedication and hard work and there is no shortcut to it." I teach others as much as I can, and I also feel happy when they could give suggestions and advice without any inhibition to enable me to do better in my work. We learn continuously from our mistakes or those of others,' says Dr Kesava Mannur, a leading surgeon based out of London, who had served as the director of Bariatric Surgery at Homerton University Hospital until 2017 and continues to train several surgeons in this field of surgery.

#GameofDrones

AS AN INDIVIDUAL

- I am not aware of the modus operandi in the new team I have joined; I tried to speak up a few times but didn't impress upon the team.
    - o I think I was using terminology which they did not appreciate/understand.
- I go by the public opinion that 'it is not allowed to speak here'—we just execute what we are told to and keep silent.
- I do not have a mentor in my team who helps me improve my articulation.
- I tried making a point few times and it did not go anywhere, so I gave up and kept to myself.
- I tend to get argumentative; if I believe I am correct, then I have every right to get loud and be aggressive with others.
- I do not prefer informal conversations; I only work on emails and formal meetings.

AS A LEADER

- If someone from the team speaks up out of turn in meetings, I take it as a sign of disrespect.
- I believe in hierarchical conversations; I limit my discussions with a few first-level associates who report to me.
- Information sharing needs to be strictly controlled and stifled. If team gets to know of most of the information, then I will lose my relevance.
- I am the sole representative of my team's work to the senior management or other teams.

Now discover and evaluate each roadblock. Think of it as a real drone and see how it is doing. Be honest and review how well you are flying it.

- ☐ **Fully autonomous flight**
- ☐ **Guided flights**
- ☐ **Irregular flight path**
- ☐ **Unwilling to take off**

#KeyResonatingActions

- Get familiar with the roles and the associated responsibilities in the team or unit so that you make appropriate communication with the right people.
- Check if there is a preferred mode of communication within the team (especially if you are coming in new).
- Know the agenda of different forums of the team and conventionally what kind of topics have been discussed where. For example, bringing in a grievance in an appreciation meeting or a leadership broadcast will get you a bad reputation.
- Request for a mentor. Learn the Dos and Don'ts of the place while making a point (without having to subdue your content) and if any subtleties in articulation.
- Always be kind, especially if you are right and others are wrong.
- Be mindful of the kind of topics and how you are making your points. Building a good reputation of someone who cares about the team and brings useful points will get you more attention than otherwise.

- If you made an important point which was not received well, persist with it. Ask for a one-on-one discussion with your lead or manager where it can be discussed again.
- Do not try to disrupt discussions with negativity just to gain attention and visibility.
- As a manager, invest time and effort to coach the team in 'meeting manners' and how a discussion can be run productively.
- Learn about the different expressive habits of your team. For instance, some may prefer verbal expression in forums, whereas others may be comfortable with written communication. Be a receiving/approachable leader with whom the team can share and converse.

#StickyNoteWorthy

Communication leads to community, that is, to understanding, intimacy and mutual valuing.

Rollo May

The intent to share and get a sense of contribution is a powerfully motivating aspect for every associate in a team. If this is not encouraged meaningfully, there is a risk of individuals getting into a zone of apathy, with ideas getting dried up (since there is no one to receive them) over a period of time. Constantly being part of a share (ideas) and receive (ideas and feedback) loop with the rest of the team gives a feeling of staying connected and also allows nurturing of new ideas. When this is complemented with a good culture of listening to each other, it results in a progressive environment where things get done with conviction.

13

FIST BUMP

A Corona Story

Dr Sita heard about Alvaro for the first time during her weekend shift at the John Jenkins geriatrics hospital. Fatima, her colleague, walked into the doctor's room around noon, shortly after her 'patient field trip' as she called it, for fun. 'He is one person I am sure has no real problem. You should see him act up as if he has breathing issues…,' she said and enacted the sound of a wheezing horse, 'That's how he does it the moment any doctor gets close to him.' This was not the first time Fatima made that complaint. To top it all, 'Do you think I am making up my illness?' he would scream at every duty doctor who would pay him a visit.

Shortly after his arrival into the hospital, he was shifted to Ward 52 and gained quite a reputation of being 'that big difficult guy'. 'He has a weird personal journal made from blank sides of the postal envelopes cut out and stuck to a clipper pad; he says he doesn't like wasting so much blank space there,' Agnes, the head nurse told everyone.

Dr Sita briefly studied the case sheet and, even before she met him, framed an opinion on Alvaro after listening to all the others at the hospital. She learnt that Alvaro was being kept in a dual patient room until recently but shifted to another room as they found out that the other patient tested positive for COVID. She gently knocked on the door and as she stepped into the room, she got a quick glimpse of a giant person lying calmly on the bed. But as soon as Alvaro sensed that someone was in the room, he got to his infamous 'breath difficulty' act. Dr Sita waited patiently for him to settle down and proceeded to examine him. Alvaro complained the whole time saying that there was something wrong with him and the doctors wouldn't believe him.

Alvaro was a huge guy, with a heavy build, and a height of about 6 feet 9 inches. He had flowing greyish black hair put away neatly in a ponytail. Although he was 79 years old, he barely looked 60, and perhaps his physique was a reason why he did not get empathetic treatment easily from the doctors at John Jenkins. His demeanour was also dubious, and he looked generally suspicious about everyone who approached him. He had very few belongings, in fact just two which Dr Sita noticed, his makeshift journal—several neatly cut blank envelopes tucked into a small, clipped pad—and a bedside mini catholic cross.

Dr Sita visited Alvaro several times in the following days, and each episode started with his wheezing act. However, she tried to be kind and gave him all the attention. It was perhaps her honesty, or her tiny size compared to his (she was barely 5 feet tall and quite slim), he did not find her or her words intimidating. '"Alvaro", what does it mean?' Dr Sita asked him casually during one of the visits. 'It's Spanish. It means guardian, kid,' he replied with a heavy voice in between his wheezes. 'That is very nice; you can stop wheezing now. Are you from Spain?' she asked. 'Oh no! I come from Uruguay; it is a long story. I really believe I have something in me that is waiting to get me,' he complained.

'You have been kind to me, doc; you are very nice, not like the others; I trust your smile…,' he continued and Dr Sita thought this conversation was again going towards 'Can I get another dose of cortisone?' but to her surprise, Alvaro said, 'I had a very painful life in Uruguay. It has been a life of struggle. People think I am a ruffian, or I work for a mafia or something like that.

I went to jail during a time of political unrest in Uruguay. Would you trust me if I say that I was innocent?' he pleaded. She nodded empathetically barely hiding a sense of shock underneath her calm face. 'So I am not just getting to grips with a "big difficult guy", but also someone with a criminal history,' thought Dr Sita. She didn't know if she should make something of it yet, and thought it best not to crash land to a judgement yet.

'Thank you for believing in me. I was put in jail for a very long time. Time I could have done something with my life. I was tortured—no sleep, electric shocks, burns with cigarette butts from the guards—they didn't let me sleep,' he said and paused and Dr Sita noticed a glint in the corner of his eye. 'At this ripe age, I find myself slightly comfortable here far from Uruguay, but all that pain and torture have left something painful in me. I can't be fine,' he said and started wheezing again. 'I am here, Alvaro; do not worry, I really like your personal journal; you care so much for the environment,' she said and lifted her tiny glove clad fist towards him, egging him to do a fist bump. 'What!' he paused, smiled and gently tapped her raised fist with his huge one.

This would become their concluding routine going forward. Each time, Dr Sita found something nice about him, something that he says or does, she would give him a fist bump and he would say every time, 'You are a very nice doctor, not like the others.'

Once Dr Sita gained enough trust with him, she tried to explain the side effects of cortisone and discouraged him from pushing the doctors and asking for it. She also made it a point to share with her colleagues about Alvaro, the innocent suffering man behind that weird looking giant. It helped ease her mind that much more for having judged him multiple times earlier.

As the summer of 2020 hit, the number of corona-infected cases increased dramatically, and more and more old people turned up to John Jenkins. It was one of those days when the staff were running from ward to ward, making rounds, ensuring medical routines and most importantly ensuring order. One of the nurses who were stationed around Alvaro's ward walked up to Dr Sita huffing and puffing. 'Alvaro wants you to know that he feels something is wrong with his throat; he wants only you to come and check.' 'Not this time, Agnes, I am swamped; check his vitals and ensure his lungs stay clear; I will visit him later in the day; there are too many sick people here to take care of,' said Dr Sita and rushed off without waiting for a reply.

The day went long and after staying longer than usual, Dr Sita packed for home and stepped out of the hospital. Then it hit her, 'Oh no! I promised to see him.' Cursing herself for the slip, she rushed back to Alvaro's room. He was relaxed and watching TV with his bed slightly brought up to lift his head and upper back. He was very pleased to see her, 'I knew you would come by; I have trouble in my throat,' he complained. Although Dr Sita did not believe that there was anything wrong, just for his satisfaction, she proceeded to examine, 'Okay, say aaah!' and there it was, a painful looking infection. 'Oh dear! I would not have forgiven myself if I went home without checking this,' she thought and said, 'It is minor, don't worry, I will get you the meds.' A COVID test was also prescribed.

This incident acted like yet another painful reminder of the settling prejudice. 'He looks so strong, so he should be fine, how silly of me, being a doctor,' Dr Sita thought. The COVID test came negative too and it gave Alvaro a huge relief.

After few more days, Alvaro seemed to really recover and was close to getting discharged. 'He is eating like a horse,' said Agnes smiling. 'Do not talk about him like that in front of his favourite doc,' said Fatima winking at Dr Sita. 'We have done another round of COVID tests for everyone in that ward; there were few more cases recently,' she added. The test result this time turned out to be positive for Alvaro.

It was for Dr Sita to take the tough news to him. 'But it was negative just recently,' he expressed his shock, 'Am I going to die? How long do I have? How serious is it?' he was panic stricken. 'Now! Don't worry so much, Alvaro; your symptoms are mild; you will recover very well. See all those older people going home? It would be the same with you; very soon we will send you home,' she smiled. 'You are not making this up to make me feel good, doc?' he asked sadly. 'You have such a beautiful cross; you should have more faith, don't worry,' she said and made him do a reluctant fist bump. 'We will have to shift you to the corona ward; you will be taken care of; I will come and visit you often,' she promised. 'Can you please get me my own room? No one feels comfortable around me,' he pleaded. 'I will try; don't lose hope,' she said. 'Can you please get me a bag for me to carry my things…?' he spoke heavily, 'Please give me a paper bag, no plastic.' Her respect for him went up several notches again. Despite of his state of mind and situation, he still showed that he cared. Dr Sita didn't realize then that it would be her last fist bump opportunity with him. 'Of course, we will get you that,' she said and left with a smile.

Dr Sita's health deteriorated the very next day and she was the next one to fall for the famed virus. It was a while before she could head back to John Jenkins. After the initial greetings and exchange of kind remarks from colleagues and the chief, she turned around to ask Fatima, 'How is Alvaro doing? I should go check on him, it has been a while.' She did not reply and instead nudged Dr Sita to check his case file. Shortly after he was shifted to the corona ward, Alvaro's health deteriorated; he was shifted to acute ward where he struggled but refused to take any advanced treatment. The final comments said, 'It reminds me of my torture in Uruguay, I don't want it!' After a couple of days of struggle, he went into a coma and never came back.

It took a while for this to sink in to Dr Sita. It is not unusual for her to face death in her profession and being in the geriatrics ward meant that more often than not she would be greeted with the ultimate truth of life. However, the interactions with Alvaro stirred up something completely different. She wondered what really killed Alvaro—a life of prejudice and mistreatment or a brief stint with the virus?

#WorkplaceWhispers

While diversity has become part of the CEO strategy in most organizations, the aspect of discrimination (most subtle to most crude) exists in the workplace and continues to be one of the top causes of stress for the associates. Although the situation has broadly improved in most organizations, and globalization has ensured a broader outlook in general, one needs to be mindful of the subtle biases at work and practise being empathetic and understanding.

THE GREAT FEELING OF BEING UNDERSTOOD

In one of my overseas assignment, I fondly recollect one of my key customers often asking, 'I would like to understand the background of the associates working for me from your organization—their context, how they would like to be addressed, what they dislike, when is the best time to make a request and how I should make a point. I want them to know that I understand them and appreciate them very much.' He would do this elaborate preparation before every meeting with the team and try his best to make a connect. And it worked every time!

'Most conflicts in a workplace are based out of assumptions of "malicious intent" from the other person. And they die down as soon as one takes a step forward to make an honest attempt to connect. It has always worked for me; it is very tough for someone to misunderstand me and vice versa. I speak my heart out and expect nothing less,' says Suresh Deshpande, an accomplished business leader. 'Also giving a feeling of "don't worry, I understand you" is a great enabler coming from a leader to his team, especially during stressful times,' he adds.

THE CIRCLE OF FEAR: AN ANALOGY FROM ANIMAL KINGDOM

'Every animal has a "circle of fear" or "locus of comfort". It is critical to understand at what distance that line exists and not cross it. You will see that if this line is not crossed, the animals are in their most natural state, and this is what every wildlife photographer wants, to capture the moments when they are natural. If the line is crossed, then the animals get into flight or fight. It needs to be respected at all costs. There are also several nuances and patterns of behaviour, and if one is patient, a bond can be established with the subject (bird or animal), then you can take stunning photos,' says A. Srikanth, a wildlife photographer and a program manager at Microsoft.

While not as sensitive and marked as with the animal kingdom, there is a 'line'/locus of comfort at an individual level too. Treading this 'line' carefully and interacting with respect at all times with patience and tolerance ensures that a good connect (bond) is established between each other. Based on one's diversity factor (as discussed in Chapter 21), there are individual behaviours and nuances which one tends to carry to the workplace. As individuals, and particularly as leaders, one needs to be mindful of this, making a consistent choice to side with empathy every time.

Andrei Jacob hails from a remote town of Poland and is extremely skilful but also timid. He displays a behaviour of being overtalkative while under stress and goes silent in an aggressive environment. Robert Alb is an assertive go-getter manager who is driven by results and gets impatient in conversations. Andrei joins the team of Robert as a database engineer.

It is a common sight during team meetings where Robert does hard reviews and gets into a conflict situation with Andrei. Andrei starts with being overtalkative and unclear with his responses, infuriating Robert further and making him aggressive, in turn driving Andrei to get into a muted shell. Robert always subsequently apologizes to Andrei in private. Within few months, Andrei quits the team unable to build a working rapport with Robert.

There are individuals hailing from a variety of backgrounds and exhibit different response times. Some are not very fluent in English (or other workplace language), struggle to express and get treated improperly under the pressure of time and expectation to be 'on the toes'.

THE LOCAL LANGUAGE COMPULSION

It isn't done deliberately, but if you ever have been part of a group that speaks a different language (or even attended meetings where you are in single-digit minority), then you have experienced the 'compulsive local language' treatment. All of a sudden, conversations erupt in a dialect that you can't catch despite your best facial expressions and hidden nervous strain. It usually takes a couple of minutes in formal environments, and forever in informal ones, before the rest of the group realizes that there is someone struggling to keep up, and switch gears back to English.

CANNOT CATCH ME ALL THE TIME

One of the common elements of stress to the associates is when your colleagues/customers take your availability for granted, at all times. This makes one feel like a commodity and undermines one's productivity. However, you will be surprised to note the support you get when preferences are shared openly. For instance, without looking at the calendar, my team can tell at what times I will most certainly not answer the call, when I tend to start work and how my work patterns are. And vice versa! Over a period of time, I have learnt the working habits of my team (not only by asking them but also by observing them keenly) and what kind of topics should be discussed at what times of the day with them. Although this takes some effort, it helps drive mutual respect and get things done with least conflict and hiccups.

#GameofDrones

- I tend to have strong opinions against certain individuals at the workplace based on their background.
- I am not aware of or mindful of preferences in interaction with my colleagues. I don't mind disturbing them at any time.
- I believe in the idea that one should leave their cultural background at home while coming to workplace. Once at work, we should all conform to same behaviours.
- I dislike those who do not mingle in the same way as the others and behave preferentially (food or social habits).
- I tend to lay low and not participate with others as I feel awkward about my eating preferences.
- My lack of fluency in language makes me hide my ideas and avoid being visible in team meetings.
- I am afraid that my manager might feel bad so I accept everything that gets pushed down on me; it causes a lot of stress but I don't speak about it.
- As a manager, I am not sensitive to the background or habits of my team members; all I focus on and care about is results.

- I expect the team to take my requests as their highest priority, as I know what is best for all of us.

Now discover and evaluate each roadblock. Think of it as a real drone and see how it is doing. Be honest and review how well you are flying it.

- [ ] **Fully autonomous flight**
- [ ] **Guided flights**
- [ ] **Irregular flight path**
- [ ] **Unwilling to take off**

#KeyResonatingActions

- Find opportunities to get to know your colleagues better in informal settings.
- Encourage forums where background, behaviours, strengths and practices can be openly shared and respected by all.
- Especially be open to share your behaviours and how you tend to respond under stress. For instance, few people absolutely hate to be interrupted during a presentation and take questions towards the end.
- Be explicit and proud about your speaking habits and difficulties, if any. Language is certainly an important medium, but skills and attitude got you the job that you have (assuming you are not in a speech-primary-skill job like helpdesk support).
- Be accommodative; learn about the work patterns, personal preferences and practices of your colleagues and team; and work around with them. You will be rewarded with loyalty and great productivity.

- Be mindful to say 'thank you' and 'sorry' often—taking colleagues for granted and being hurtful (even unintentionally so) are major turn-offs.
- Have a goal to bring a smile to at least a couple (go for a higher count thou noble heart!) of colleagues at workplace, by doing or saying something nice.

#StickyNoteWorthy

Manners are a sensitive awareness of the feelings of others. If you have that awareness, you have good manners, no matter what fork you use.

Emily Post

Derailers of discrimination based on one's physique, dialect, cultural background, personal practices, work habits and so on need to be fought diligently with tolerance and rapt mindfulness. While this is yet another leadership calling for every sincere leader to embrace diversity—cognitive or physical—it is a responsibility of each and every individual at workplace to lead by example and constantly bring smiles to each other.

14 THE ENEMY AROUND

This tale dates back to the 8th century BC in an ancient monastery situated in the ranges of Mount Hido of Japan, much before the dawn of the Samurai. Legend has it that the monastery was home to monks with great knowledge and was run by a sensei who could wield the ultimate weapon, the Sword of Hido. Several warriors of Japan and foreign lands approached the monastery to train with the sensei and attempt wielding the Hido, but the sword would allow only the one 'that had no enemies'. The sensei had no match, and he was rumoured to be as old as Mount Hido itself. He was also a teacher of great skill in calligraphy, philosophy and other arts and selflessly taught whoever approached him earnestly.

One day, three warriors from different monasteries of Japan approached the monastery of Hido. 'We offer respects from our monasteries, Sensei Akito,' the warriors bowed, 'We have each vanquished all the warriors from the east, west and south of Japan and have come here on the orders of our senseis to conquer "the Sword of Hido", with your permission,' they spoke in unison. 'First you must rest, I will meet you in front of the shoro (*bell tower*) tomorrow before the dawn,' said Akito. 'Hai, sensei!' they bowed.

The next morning, students and monks of the Hido monastery gathered in the arena in front of the bell tower. 'We welcome the warriors Goro from the eastern monastery, Akira from the western monastery and Hiroshi from the southern monastery. Before we see their skill and begin their training, today we also bid farewell to Kiyoshi—the finest—as he moves on to conquer the next challenge of his life...,' said Sensei Akito, 'May you continue to challenge and *conquer the undesirables*,' Akito wished. Kiyoshi bowed to the sensei in gratitude and took leave from the monastery. Akito then turned to the new warriors.

'To what extent would you train to achieve the impossible? Do you have what it takes to conquer the Sword of Hido!' he demanded. 'Hai! Sensei' they said. 'Between the three of us we have vanquished every great warrior of the land; we will fight each other and with the finest of your monastery to rid ourselves of all our enemies,' said Goro. 'I will take on your pride first, Goro,' challenged Akira. 'I will duel with whichever of you survive,' said Hiroshi. 'Alas! The finest of the monastery just departed from here in his new quest,' smiled Akito. 'We could follow him and challenge him, sensei; we await your orders,' the warriors spoke. Ignoring their request, Akito held up an ancient-looking sword which seemed hidden under his long robes, 'Behold the Hido!' he said.

Akito held the sword with his left hand on its sheath and called out to each of them one after the other. 'Step forth, Goro, and hold the hilt, do not let go until I say so,' ordered Akito and closed his eyes. As Giro touched the sword, a searing pain shot through his arm and through the entire body; the pain was unbearable, but the warrior held on. 'Hmm, *anger, greed, overeating* ... hahaha ... let go!' 'Now, Akira!' he said and the ritual was repeated. '*No mercy, ruthlessness, pride, oversleeping* ... aha ... let go!.' 'Step forth, Hiroshi.... This is a strange one ... *lack of respect for scriptures* ... *fear of public speaking* ... *stealing relics* ...

hmmm … let go.' The warriors were in pain but stood resolute in their positions.

'Well done! You have exhibited forbearance. Here is what you shall do in your attempt to conquer the Hido.

Goro: You shall be fed one meal a day; You shall spend the day teaching your technique to the students and monks of this monastery; leave no trick hidden from them and share all you have got.

Akira: There is a ghost of a great warrior trapped in a nearby cave; you will fight him and attempt to defeat him. You will fight him in the night and return to the monastery at daybreak.

Hiroshi: You will read the scriptures of the monastery and lecture the monks and students, morning and evening. You shall spend the day cleaning the relics of the Pagoda,' said Akito.

The warriors were shocked with the tasks given by the sensei. No real fight, except for Akira who was to face a ghost! They did not understand but chose to follow the sensei. Akira spoke up steadily, 'Sensei! It is an honour to fight the ghost warrior. In my monastery, we either kill or die in a fight. How can I kill a ghost!' he asked. 'Hoshi is tough to beat! He is never beaten! But you may try your mettle,' replied Akito. 'Then I pay you my last respects, sensei, I shall die with pride,' said Akira. 'We shall see, we will take the ritual every full-moon day and let Hido test your worthiness,' announced Akito.

The three warriors left to tend to their chores. Goro was fed half a meal and had to spend all day teaching the students what he had learnt so far in his life. 'My code of honour prevents me from killing all of you for attempting to steal my knowledge,' he would yell in rage, but reminding himself of his task, he would attempt to share, although in extreme discomfort.

Hiroshi found it impossible to speak up in front of the gathering and could barely stand up in shame all through the lecture routine. His hands could not restrain themselves in stealing the relics from the Pagoda, but he promptly returned them to their place the next day. Akira had the worst fate of them all. The ghost Hoshi was impossible to beat. 'You think you are merciless in battle; let me show you how it is done,' Hoshi would attack in a fit of rage and vehemence. However, he would not strike the death blow. 'Please have mercy and kill me,' Akira would plead, but Hoshi would laugh and with a sadistic tone say, 'Come back tonight, warrior, I need to creep back into my crypt.' 'Oh please! I cannot go back to the monastery fallen, I cannot commit suicide, please…,' Akira would plead, but Hoshi would not budge.

The warriors struggled with their tasks and soon it was time again to face the ritual. The pain of the ritual was unbearable. Akito said, 'I congratulate you for failing every day. Goro, you cannot cheat the sword; you have to give all you have got and share everything you have learnt. Hiroshi, do you have enough determination to face your fears and restrain your instincts? Akira, are you beginning to learn the importance of being merciful?' he demanded. 'Hai, sensei!' came the reply. 'Good! Hido will trial you on the next full-moon day,' said Akito.

Over the next several seasons, the ritual continued every full-moon day. The warriors were resolute. 'We shall die here but will not return to our monasteries as failures,' they said.

Goro learnt over a period of time the joy of sharing. As and when he remembered something, he would run after the students and monks to teach every single trick and learning he had received. 'I find a greater sense of joy in giving than taking; I don't feel the need for food also so much, sensei,' he would remark.

Hiroshi offered to help some of the monks with their chores in return for their private time in helping him with public speaking. He gradually learnt to overcome his fear and also gathered a lot of learning from the scriptures of the monastery.

'I feel indebted to you, sensei; I would like to continue on my path of learning,' he said.

Akira died several hundred times without actually dying. His pride was crushed, and he repented for his merciless acts as a warrior. But he also practised over time and developed great skills. 'Your demeanour is not so arrogant anymore,' Hoshi said one day before the fight, 'but I will still enjoy crushing you warrior,' he smiled. 'I feel bad for you, Hoshi; I forgive you,' said Akira. A brilliant fight ensued, and Akira disarmed Hoshi before dawn. 'I am defeated!' said Hoshi. 'No! You have been a great teacher; thank you for teaching me all these days, sensei; I bow to you,' said Akira. In a swift breeze, Hoshi departed from the cave.

'Warriors! You have now conquered your real enemies—pride, lack of mercy, covetousness, oversleeping, overeating, lack of respect, anger—*the enemies that lie within.* Hido may accept you now,' he smiled. Overjoyed by their victory and enlightenment, they asked, 'Is that it, sensei? Are we now the greatest warriors of the land?' 'Hido helped you divine an important truth, one that every warrior should assimilate within—*of the real enemy, the real undesirable in oneself.* But there are greater truths to be learnt, and you will continue the journey. *As you attempt to learn higher truths, you should attempt to let go more and more of your undesirables within which hinder you from knowing them.* But yes, you are indeed the finest warriors of the land. May you continue to challenge and conquer the undesirables,' wished Akito.

#WorkplaceWhispers

There is a two-pronged conflict/dilemma around opportunities that one gets into constantly at the workplace, either as an individual or as a team: (a) you think that you have the skill/competence, but others (usually the opportunity providers) don't quite think so and you end up losing out or (b) you do not think that you have the skills/competence, but the external parties think otherwise and expect you to get the job done.

In both the conflicts, (a) there are aspects which you can control and those which you cannot, (b) there are positive choices you can make vs give up on the situation or be led into a wrong direction and (c) there are learnings to be noted for facing such conflicts in the future vs sticking to your beliefs and not learn anything new.

THE WAILING WALL: WHAT YOU CANNOT CONTROL

Consider Figure 14.1, which illustrates the importance of learning about a problem and focusing on what one can control.

Depending upon the magnitude of the work environment you are part of (or the nature of work), there will be tough

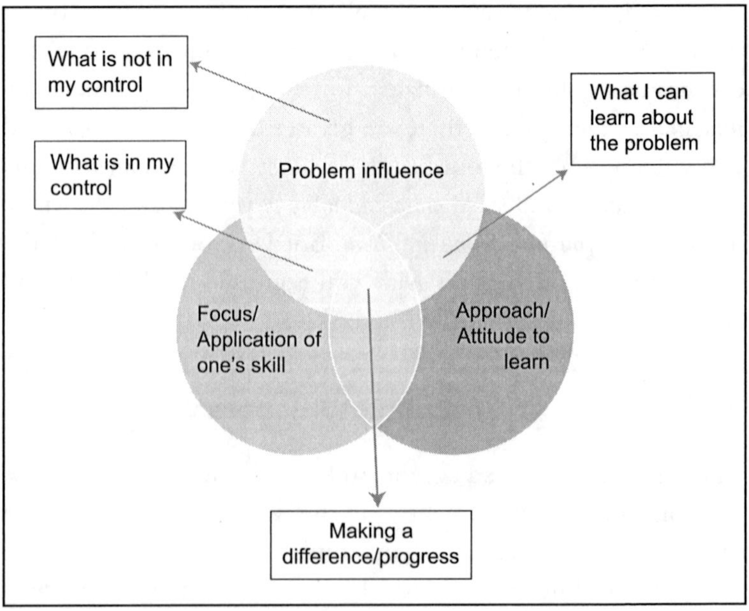

Figure 14.1 Approaching a Problem

and sometimes explosive problems. One of my mentors, Mr Emmanuel David, Head of Tata Management Training Centre, was recollecting his conversations with a renowned heart surgeon from Pune, India, and the 'mission critical' nature of the heart surgeries. 'What is interesting to note is how the specialists approach the problem vs commoners. Their knowledge/ experience draws them to look at what is the next best step in improving the condition before the surgery is done or to prepare the patient to be in the best form for the surgery. They will not so much worry about hundred negative things which will kill the patient (while they are definitely aware of those) but focus on one thing which can improve the condition, and they do this progressively,' he adds.

This is true in any field with varying degrees of 'mission criticality'. And the approach one takes when hit with a problem is also common in most fields. The knowledgeable/experienced ones tend to be mindful of hundred things which are wrong about the situation but focus on the one thing which they can fix, whereas the inexperienced ones tend to get blocked at their own wailing wall: 'but this is unfair, I deserve to get this opportunity…' or 'they don't understand, I know better….' Reaching out to discuss, taking actions in the areas which one can control and making progress are always better alternatives in overcoming the wall.

LEARNING ON THE MOVE: CONQUERING THE UNDESIRABLES

Seeking to learn, gain a clear and deep understanding of a subject, and being thoroughly prepared in all scenarios are the hallmarks of a leader.

One of the senior leaders in TCS, V. Rajanna, always carries a book and a pen with him to all meetings and never hesitates to note key points. He openly seeks clarifications in meetings, even those with large participation, without a thought about his role or seniority. He prepares thoroughly and, where required, seeks help from SMEs irrespective of their role or experience. And, of course, he expects that his team is thoroughly prepared too. 'Rajanna looks for details and clarity, and we must go thoroughly prepared about each aspect being discussed. We cannot be fluffy' is a common remark that is made when we prepare for meetings with him.

His style of extraordinary preparation and seeking help from anyone around him inspires us to believe that *facing one's undesirable (the real enemy) without hesitation is the first step towards conquering it.*

FEEDBACK AND FEED-FORTH: LEARNING FROM CONFLICTS

One (or a team) could land with any of the following situations often despite best efforts to rectify the expectation mismatch:

- *Opportunity is lost:* Your manager/customer does not believe you can do the job as you could not persuade them in time or identify and fix your gaps (undesirables).
- *Opportunity is thrust upon and there is a failure in execution:* Your manager/customer thought that you could do it, but you did not understand the nature of their expectations and went on with execution (with your gaps and lack of conviction).
- *Opportunity is thrust upon and you succeed:* Your manager/customer thought that you could do it, you did not understand why they thought so and there is accidental success (somehow things worked out!).

Whichever might be the case, it is important to have a thorough retrospect (usually best to do it as close to the milestone as possible) and take/provide feedback. 'It is particularly important to know why we succeeded and learn to replicate it. Failures tend to be much more visible,' says Keshav Varma, a senior business leader and mentor.

#GameofDrones

- I often find myself resenting about an opportunity lost; I don't think this place and these people understand my situation.
- I am not aware of my shortcomings and areas of improvement. I tend to get feedback occasionally but I am usually not convinced about it.
- I have a good view of my shortcomings, and I am also aware of gaps of others around me, but they seem to go ahead all the time.
- Although I know the areas of improvement, the effort it would take to overcome them is quite a lot. I am not sure if it will be worth the while to invest so much time.
- Although we do not have all the resources/skills, we keep succeeding as a team somehow and we are not quite sure of the formula of our success.
- I find it awkward to take help from others, especially juniors in the team.
- As a manager I hide the organizational constraints or my own constraints from the team; they may see this as my weakness and show me less respect.

Now discover and evaluate each roadblock. Think of it as a real drone and see how it is doing. Be honest and review how well you are flying it.

- [ ] **Fully autonomous flight**
- [ ] **Guided flights**
- [ ] **Irregular flight path**
- [ ] **Unwilling to take off**

#KeyResonatingActions

- Find a friend at work with whom you could openly discuss your gaps and ask for no-nonsense feedback on where you should improve.
- Identify a mentor (or more per area of improvement) who could help put together an improvement plan.
- Publish your goals and milestones to your mentor or closed group of friends who can constantly nudge you and keep you going.
- Constantly strive to gain expertise in your area of work, especially on potential failure points and how to go about fixing them.
- Invite feedback and make it a habit to seek feedback after every occurrence of an action in the area where you would like to improve (e.g., if you would like to improve in conducting audits, invite a senior auditor to observe you in action and provide feedback).
- Jointly reflect as a team to evaluate the methods being followed and look for weak spots/improvement areas.

#StickyNoteWorthy

Golf is a game that is played on a five-inch course—the distance between your ears.

Bobby Jones

Along with having a sensei (mentor/friend) at work who can keep an eye on you and constantly feed you with positive and uplifting narratives, it is important to be disciplined about the internal narrative which is allowed in the mind—what you choose to focus on. And while it is important to be sensitive to the challenges and the expectations (fair or unfair) around, it should not distract focus from tackling the 'undesirable' which exists in one's control/vicinity. When this is done at a team level, it progressively takes down the real enemies (constraints which can be overcome) at work, helps to replicate success and makes it more predictable.

15

SEEK OR SPEAK

Sandeep was an orphan young man in the village of Grayhills and made a living by delivering the produce from his village to the nearby towns and villages. He grew up as that 'dull lad with speaking difficulties' but with 'busy legs'. Everyone wanted to send him 'off on the next errand', and he did not mind that at all.

While the villagers made him to work for them, they always teased him for his stutter. Sandeep was upset about not being able to ever speak a sentence; everyone was always in a rush and would not let him finish, except for his old friend at the temple located on the very edge of the dangerous northern forest. Sandeep would go to this old man and talk to him whenever his tired legs needed some rest and tired mind some solace. The old man never interrupted and listened patiently. He would occasionally say, 'In whatever you do, do good. But when you lose all hope, take to the north.' It never made sense to Sandeep.

One day, Sandeep couldn't take it any longer. He rushed to the temple to tell the old man that he will leave this village. But to his dismay, the old man was gone without a trace. Sandeep wondered if an animal from the northern forest got to his old fellow. Resolute not to go back to the village, he boldly stepped into the forest.

Quickly enough he was in the middle of a dense forest and it was night time. Panic stricken and sad, Sandeep cursed himself for having left the protection of the village and sat under a huge banyan tree.

'I am glad you had faith on my words despite your frustrations and fears,' came a familiar voice which made Sandeep jump in his place. 'Don't be afraid; this is your old friend,' spoke the voice which seemed to be coming from a dark silhouette sitting next to Sandeep. 'Is he a ghost? What is he doing here?' thought Sandeep, still in shock and unable to speak. 'Not really, I am not a ghost. I am the residing deity of the northern forests. I move around this place. What do you wish son?' the voice sounded reassuring, although Sandeep felt his heartbeat getting only faster, in fear.

'I wish to reverse my place; I want to be ahead of the world; I want to be recognized as the smartest; I want your ability to listen to unstated ideas; and I want to overcome my stammer,' cried Sandeep, this time he felt he spoke without a stutter. 'Are you sure? Do you want to find a place by turning against the world? So be it,' said the old man and with what appeared to be a soft gush of wind, the silhouette flew away into the forest, 'Keep going north' was what Sandeep heard before he fainted under the tree.

Sandeep woke up jolted by bright sunlight and felt a strange sense of intuition dawn upon him. 'Was that a dream? Did I encounter a ghost? what happened to me?' his eyes locked with the ones of a pigeon sitting on a nearby branch. 'I wouldn't know, but the nearest village is still quite far; you should keep moving; there are wild animals around here,' the bird flew away. 'I must have surely gone mad. Did I just hear a bird's thoughts?!!!' but he moved ahead in the direction pointed by the bird and after several days of walking and strange encounters with several animals which seemed to share their thoughts with him, he reached what seemed like the edge of a human dwelling.

Sandeep quickly realized that his stammer was gone, and he had supernatural abilities to discern unstated thoughts and ideas from those around. It didn't take long before his fame spread as a fast thinker and a very wise man. He could solve most problems; all he had to do was gaze deeply and the answers came to him from those around, including the animals and birds. His reputation landed him a place with the king's court. He finally felt accomplished, but not satisfied. 'Where is the fun in beating the village folk? I should be considered the smartest of all in the king's court,' he told himself.

And it appeared to work that way. Sandeep was the quickest to respond in any conversation. No one matched his ability to converse and share ideas quickly, which were being dug out from their innermost minds, without their knowledge. The king showered praises on Sandeep, 'You are a gift to my court; you are the smartest living man on the planet.' While the courtiers silently appreciated Sandeep along with the king, they could not fathom his abilities. 'I had exactly the same ideas, but Sandeep was quicker,' said one. 'The other day, I thought I had the king's attention, but the thought flew out of my mind, as if someone extracted it and gave it to Sandeep,' said another. 'Maybe he is just smart and we are losing our skills,' said one of the senior courtiers.

In a short time, two things gained 'loud' prominence in the king's court: Sandeep's voice and his arrogance. 'Do we need so many courtiers when I am here to take care of the proceedings?' he joked around. The courtiers slowly lost their confidence, with the king not paying attention to what was happening and promoting Sandeep to the role of chief minister. Slowly and steadily, they started losing interest in the affairs of the kingdom: 'Sandeep will take care anyway,' they told themselves as they slipped slowly into inaction and indifference.

One day the court faced a serious challenge. The kingdom got into trade issues with a powerful kingdom called Cryseilles.

The king knew very well that Cryseilles was mighty and getting into conflict with them was not an option. This needed to be resolved immediately. He turned to Sandeep for ideas. Sandeep frantically looked around the court to sense ideas from around. The trade minister was least interested and so were the other courtiers. The king gave an ultimatum to Sandeep to fix the problem in a week's time or they would all have to face dire circumstances.

'Did the power fade away? What just happened today?' Sandeep quickly looked around and found a cat crossing the street. 'If only I could be the best cat, all cats should think highly of me; why should I go looking for food? I must be the king of cats,' purred the cat as it entered a nearby house. 'Poor thing! It doesn't know what it's asking for,' Sandeep thought. So I do have the power, but then why did I not hear anyone in the court.

As he paced frantically in the middle of the night without sleep, he remembered his old friend, 'What did you make of my life?' he spoke loudly. 'I warned you,' came a soft reply carried by a gush of wind blowing into the room through the open window. Sandeep found the old man sitting on his bed smiling. 'Your powers were pure, but you used them to outsmart others, to be distinct yourself, while everyone around you suffered,' he said, 'Looks like you achieved what you wanted to, son; you gave the world a taste of your previous life, didn't you now?'

'I didn't know it would lead to this, but help me understand what happened; why don't I hear the courtiers anymore? They were so smart before,' pleaded Sandeep. 'Indeed, they were … until you came by. To create an upward spiral for yourself, you sent them spiralling down, and they have no more ideas for you to steal … quickly,' said the old man. 'This is not what I wanted; my anger drove me mad; please help me, old friend; can I do anything to restore the balance which I have disturbed?' cried Sandeep. 'You diverted the channels of inspiration and appreciation out from everyone else, towards yourself. It helped in the short term but also created a deeper damage. Reverse the flow, son; help the ones around you get what you have always wanted—"appreciation for what they are". So far you chose to "speak" ahead of the others, now "seek" to help others speak. Do you think you want to do that?' the old man gazed intently. 'Yessssss,' stuttered Sandeep. 'So be it,' said a parting soft gush of wind.

Sandeep's stammer returned, but it didn't matter to him as he didn't try so much to speak. He reversed his ability to gently inspire people around him to find their inner voice. In his presence, the courtiers felt that their abilities were suddenly amplified. They recollected their experience and wisdom and shared it freely with each other. The king realized his mistake and paid attention to them, thanks to the inspiration from Sandeep. Sandeep was no longer the chief minister, but he was retained in the court as someone who took note of the proceedings.

Sandeep enjoyed his new role. He did not have to speak, and he had plenty of time and a bubbling heart filled with the desire to 'seek' and inspire people around him.

#WorkplaceWhispers

Speed is fanciful. Most of us grew in environments where rapid responses were rewarded and solving problems quickly sought appreciations from teachers and impressed (or depressed, but we were fine with that too!) fellow students. When it comes to a workplace teeming with diversity, 'idolizing speed' at the cost of 'harnessing collaboration' may not be a smart option.

While being rapid and sharp with responses might be an edge, and even essential in certain contexts, it should not become a dominant behaviour of the team where certain individuals are always ignored because of their speed or their dialect or inability to speak as cleanly as the others.

'TEAM MEETINGS OR EXTEMPORE COMPETITIONS?'

In my experience of running a number of team meetings and participating in as many of those as a team member, I have noticed the following: associates (regardless of age in the organization) who cherish visibility or want to be heard more than the others tend to occupy the hotspots in the room. And the others, with apathy, hesitation, spirit of generosity or self-imposed constraints tend to happily sacrifice the hotspots consistently!

And I used to be in the former group for a decent time, never bothering to look at whose other voices I was stubbing out by being the loudest in the room.

PROXIMITY AFFECT

One of our group leaders who I worked with earlier had this habit—once everybody settled into the meeting room, he would take a good look at the gathering and deliberately move people around. Those who he knew did not have a hesitation to speak or are familiar, he would ask them to move slightly away and invite the newcomers or the ones with lesser-words-per-minute ability to come closer. 'Let them first get comfortable being close to the leader, eventually they will open up,' he would say.

MATTER OF GOOD WORDS PER MINUTE

With the work cultures shifting gradually to remote work (for good or not-so-good reasons) and on-demand online collaboration, the visible hotspots are gone, but then it is even more challenging to maintain the tempo of the meeting with interactions getting swayed by dominant individuals. Here is where the onus on the leader/anchor of the meetings is even higher and using a language and pace which would make everyone on the call comfortable is important. Each interaction is an opportunity to accentuate the behaviours which promote collaboration, rather than those which drive the majority of the team away. 'We won't be heard or understood; my leader anyway talks to his chosen few smart people' is a dangerous impression which should not be allowed to settle in the minds of the associates.

Identifying such associates who are not forthright in communication and making a connect in an environment which is less overbearing help.

#Can you reflect on the names of some of the associates in your team who are not forthright in communication but intelligent and thoughtful?

#GameofDrones

AS AN INDIVIDUAL

- I have ideas, sometimes better than the ones being discussed, but I keep them to myself or share with friends later.
- I have a different accent and cannot speak as fast as my colleagues, and I don't think anyone misses me in the discussions.
- When it comes to answering questions or expressing opinions, I am very aggressive; it is very hard for the others to make their point when I decide to speak.
- It doesn't matter if others do not understand the acronyms or complex words I use; I think my boss gets it, and that's fine.
- I heard that asking questions is the best way to draw attention of management; I ask maximum number of questions, whether others like it or not.
- I enjoy building up on the thought of others; I innovate on the fly, even by interrupting what they have to say.

AS A LEADER

- I tend to interact only with a few associates in the team (during team interactions) with whom I feel comfortable; we understand each other better.
- During key discussions, I tend to call out the names of one or two key associates all the time. If I don't take their explicit opinion, they might feel bad. I can safely ignore others.
- I do not take the effort to be understood. I expect the team to grow into learning my style. I enjoy being understood only by a few smart individuals.
- I expect rapid answers and get turned off if someone takes more time to respond; it just means that they are not good enough.

Now discover and evaluate each roadblock. Think of it as a real drone and see how it is doing. Be honest and review how well you are flying it.

☐ **Fully autonomous flight**

☐ **Guided flights**

☐ **Irregular flight path**

☐ **Unwilling to take off**

#KeyResonatingActions

AS AN INDIVIDUAL

- Build a reputation of being a team player.
- Be helpful to colleagues and try to be a catalyst in encouraging others during team interactions.
- Ask for the agenda of the meeting/discussion and prepare in advance.

- Write down a few summary items as ideas for discussion—I have found it useful to note down the points which I want to bring up prior to the meetings, as much as possible.
- Appreciate participation, especially new or usually muffled voices in the group.
- Appreciate the good work done by silent individuals who won't speak for themselves.

AS A LEADER

- Connect with the associates off the meetings and build rapport.
  - o Seek their inputs with enthusiasm and appreciation.
  - o Keenly observe the tempo and language which they tend to absorb easily, and use that knowledge while running larger forums/meetings.
- Solicit ideas on how to run larger forums.
- Learn about the activities of your team and individual context as much as possible prior to the meetings and use this knowledge to ask pointed questions to help them open up and contribute to the forum.
  - o For example, 'Uma, I know that you have performed a complex task last week, must have been an experience worth remembering? Or forgetting?'
- Maintain a friendly and approachable profile. If the barrier to contribute is very high, then associates will choose the easier option and stay calm.
- While this may not be easy all the time, especially when domain know-how is involved, practise simple language and do not assume that associates know what you are talking about.

- Encourage active listening in team meetings, instead of tuning in a preferential ear to select few—moderate effectively.

#StickyNoteWorthy

Listening is a magnetic and strange thing, a creative force. The friends who listen to us are the ones we move toward. When we are listened to, it creates us, makes us unfold and expand.

Karl A. Menniger

Trying to be the smartest in the room might look attractive to start with, but in the long run, if this turns into disregard for others, the smart one becomes the lonely one and collaboration takes a hit. The leader of the team must ensure that everyone gets to wear their thinking/expressing hats constantly so that when a crisis hits, there are more individuals with empathy and ideas to lend helping hands. And when this becomes an active pursuit of every individual of the team to help a colleague participate better, it leads to a great working environment to which the team rushes in everyday to contribute and discover their potential.

16 JUMP WITH YOU

It was one of those days when Daniel needed consultation from his colleague and best friend John over something which was bothering him at work. Both of them held senior roles in a large organization which manufactured industrial equipment.

'Overseeing yet another transformation, I sometimes feel these "transformative" changes have to stop and let us breathe. We will kill ourselves with these constant changes, the guys sitting in that corner office should plan better…,' Daniel walked in visibly frustrated. 'Good change never killed anybody, pal. How is the new set-up coming along? Have a seat,' John welcomed his friend in his office.

'In summary, it's a personal mess. I was doing well in research and now taking over this bigger team with all these new people. People management is not my thing as you know, John,' said Daniel. 'Told you before, don't fret over the term "people management" too much; focus instead on *your own conviction in the purpose* which you are trying to drive and how well you communicate it,' John smiled.

'Easy for you to say that, John, with your experience with people; I on the other hand have been dealing with machines more. Upgrading the assembly line with these new machines I thought would be a cake walk; I have done these things before, but this one is way bigger…,' Daniel continued to express the challenges with the change management involved in the huge programme which he was overseeing, '…contracting issues, thanks for your timely help there by the way, procedure compliance, quality checks, compatibility, safety, new data specifications and protocols…. I can go on…,' Daniel paused to take a sip of tea offered by John.

'And you have a highly qualified team which knows most of this stuff, don't you? What really is troubling you, my friend?' John gazed intently at Daniel.

'I can't put my finger on it; most of these guys are PHDs from top schools and very strong individuals. We are moving stuff forward; it is a long programme, but I don't get a sense that it is coming together. I wish people could just trust me more…,' said Daniel, 'I don't get the sense of having genuine conversations and overseeing trustworthy plans, John; we might or might not deliver and this is a big deal for our company's success!' he completed.

'You need a break, Dan; you've been working too hard; how's Ginny doing?' John tried to change the subject. 'She is okay; we haven't had an adventure in some time now,' replied Daniel. 'Let's take a short trip next week, Dan, along with Ginny. I want you to meet someone, and it might answer some of your questions.'

A week later: 'Uncle John, you promised me a surprise when we started, but it is boring here. I want to get back home,' the 12-year-old Ginny was sitting in the sofa along with her nanny in the hotel lobby. Ginny had a minor leg deformity by birth, limiting her ability to run or take to active sports. 'Tomorrow, Ginny; you have to trust me on this one…,' smiled John, 'Tomorrow, Dan,' he winked.

'Ask for Paul Ammerby when you get to the place and tell me everything when you get back, every minute detail Dan. Have fun Ginny,' said John as he placed a card in the hands of Dan which read sky sport with its address. 'Are you out of your mind, John? You know Ginny's situation; is this what you brought us all this way for?' Dan screamed softly turning his back to Ginny. 'Ask for Paul, and trust your friend, buddy; she will have fun; she is stronger than you think,' said John as he firmly nudged Dan back into the car, 'Remember to tell me everything when you get back, what you see and what you hear.'

'Paul is on his way, please be seated inside,' said Larry who seemed to be the one running the place. Ginny and Daniel sat in a sofa and surveyed the room. There was an equipment hanging from the ceiling which looked like training gear for sky divers, a large TV set, a couple of tables and a coffee maker. 'I am very scared, papa; do you think I can do this…?' Ginny asked Daniel as he finally explained Uncle John's grand plan to her, 'Uncle John wants you to do tandem jump, Ginny, with a person by name Paul,' he forced a smile. 'But I am scared…,' she started to say when a man walked in with a broad smile which seemed to light up the gloomy looking room. 'So was I when I took my first jump, but by the time I prepared myself to jump, I got very excited and now I have been jumping for the past 20 years,' he said as he introduced himself and shook hands, 'Hi! I am Paul and I jump off the cliffs with others for a living,' he laughed.

'Is it dangerous? What if we die?' asked Ginny. 'It is possible that sometimes the weather is rough, but then today is not the day; it looks beautiful and perfect, you will be safe,' he said, 'I know every inch of these mountains, they are my friends.' Daniel took Paul aside and tried to explain the situation with Ginny. 'If she can trot a little bit, we are good; can you run a little bit, Ginny?' he asked. 'No…,' Daniel tried to say, but 'Yes, I can run a bit,' Ginny cut in. 'Are you sure you want to do this?' Dan asked. 'I want to try, papa, I don't know,' she replied anxiously.

'I am a trainer, Mr Daniel; it is a journey to get here. First you got to get your license to paraglide on your own which takes 50 supervised independent flights and then several more to become a tandem jumper and a trainer,' Paul explained. 'There are several aspects to a great flight, the wind direction, weather conditions and so on, and we keep a track of them before we fly. But more than anything else, it is the attitude of the flyer. It is important to have fun. This is what I tell my students too. It can be quite challenging to teach them sometimes; it is important that they gain confidence quickly. But "no one has ever learned anything from an angry teacher, did they?" So I never lose patience, although if I am serious about someone not paying attention, I let them know,' he continued.

'Here let me show you some fun photos of how we create memories for life,' he said as he showed several photos and videos bursting with life and excitement to Daniel and Ginny. 'The view from up there is fantastic,' he said. 'You have to let me spend a few minutes with Ginny before I drive her up the cliff; you could wait down here and wave at us as we land, and capture some nice photos,' Paul said dancing around the place, gathering the gear needed and whistling in between. 'What makes him so lively and happy,' Daniel thought to himself. 'I love my job, and I love the place, that's why we settled here,' said Paul as if he overheard the thoughts of Dan, 'Most importantly I love my family very much, Dan, and I want to go back home alive every day for them; have no fear, your daughter is safe,' he continued to smile.

'Ginny, let me check, you have good shoes, you have warm clothes, yes, good shades, gloves, let me get you a helmet,' he rushed in and brought back a helmet, 'This should fit you well, comfy? Yeah, great, let's go.' 'What if I fall down, Paul?' asked Ginny as they drove up the cliff. 'Then I fall with you, Ginny, the equipment I have will tie us both together, but we will not fall, I fly five times every day and been flying for the last…,' '20 years,' Ginny completed with a smile. 'That's right!'

As they reached the top of the hill, Paul carefully studied the wind direction as he prepared Ginny and tethered her into the seat which connected to his and to the paraglide. 'You see that slope? We will run this way along the slope. When I tell you to run, you start running and I will run along with you, good? Oh boy, what a beautiful and bright day, we will zoom over that lake and land right in front of the place where we started, Ginny. It's time to show your dad how brave you are!' his smile was infectious and very assuring. 'Can I scream if I get scared?' Ginny asked innocently remembering her father's words, 'Be brave and don't scare Paul too much.' 'Yeaaah, you can scream and I will too, that's part of the fun; now the wind is coming right at us, time to get ready, Ginny; here we go, one, two, three … start walking … very good, a little faster, awesome, I am right behind you, you are doing great, little bit faster, woooohoooo aaaaaand we are flying….'

Ginny recounted her entire flight experience to John when they got back. 'I never screamed so much in my life before, and Paul screamed along, it was so much fun. At first I was very scared, but he was with me all along before the flight, smiling and encouraging and when he asked me to run down the slope, I was just focused on running. No one asks me to run much and I felt happy, and before I knew, I was lifted … Woooooohooooo … and we screamed,' Ginny was unstoppable and she ran around the hotel lobby reliving her experience with her arms wide open. 'Paul showed me around the big mountain, and then we zoomed over the small one, and then over the lake, and then I saw some birds flying close by; he even let me manage the lines for few minutes … and when we landed everyone was clapping and taking pictures; they made me feel special, and dad was so happy too.'

'When I grow older, I want to learn paragliding, papa, and I am going back to fly again tomorrow. Paul is great….'

'Right, Ginny, time to get you some dinner,' her nanny took her away.

'What is this all about, John? It is slowly dawning on me, but help me understand, it's your turn to speak now,' pressed Daniel. 'Elements of trust and turning fear into excitement, my friend. Paul spent may be less than 20 minutes to convince a girl with difficulty in running to jump off a cliff! Isn't that magical? What did you observe and what do you remember? It's your turn truly, not mine,' smiled John.

'I remember the smile more than anything else. As if it is plastered on his face forever, makes him feel so reassuring the moment someone looks at him,' said Daniel. 'Approachability, Dan, when you want to commit your team to jump off the cliff for you, nah, with you, the first thing they should feel is comfort being tethered to you in the first place,' John spoke gently.

Daniel moved uncomfortably in place, but eventually smiled. 'I get it, let me continue. And then the other thing I remember is how much he is vested in this sport; his life depends on him doing it well and his life depends on it in getting him back home. He is fully into it, no two thoughts and he didn't mince words mentioning it,' said Daniel. 'Conviction, Dan, if your team doesn't trust that you are fully convinced and committed about what you want them to do, it will never work. Your personal conviction as a leader is the foundation,' John reflected.

'I see where you are taking me with this, John, and I am beginning to understand. Paul then showed us pictures and videos of his previous jumps and that started getting Ginny excited; he spoke about what it takes to do what he is doing...,' Daniel said. 'Establishing credibility and visibly establishing trust. More importantly making a personal connection with the team and engaging in a dialogue,' inferred John. 'But transformations are new, and there is no past experience, John; how do you establish credibility then?' asked Daniel. 'By giving your team the feeling of flexibility and openness that we can do it together and with the collective experience, we can learn together.'

'It was great to see how Paul was making Ginny feel that it is very common to jump off the cliffs, "I do it every day with a lot of people." And how he was taking every question from Ginny very seriously, even the ones which were very naive for a 12-year-old, but given her condition,' recollected Daniel. 'Bravo! I like your sincerity in capturing these my friend. What you just narrated is much stronger than the tether that kept Ginny's and Paul's seats together—*respect*. Paul ensured that he made Ginny feel that he understood her and responded to every single question as plainly as possible. This is important to bring your team close to you, Dan,' said John.

'And we heard the rest of the story from Ginny. "What if I fall?" "I fall along with you, but I haven't had a fall in 20 years,"' recollected Daniel. 'At the end of the experience, when you hear Ginny, it is all about what she went through, what she has seen, what she has experienced, see how Paul doesn't come in the way of her experience, but guides her to have fun as much as possible. She never for once felt that she was differently abled, did she?' smiled John.

'Nope, not for a moment. Feels like I have taken the flight as much as Ginny: (a) turn fear into excitement, (b) show conviction, (c) establish trust, (d) encourage openness and willingness for joint learning, (e) respect, (f) create experiences and (g) get out of the way,' summarized Daniel as he wrote them down for his reference.

'Well, sometimes you are in the driving seat and sometimes you got to let your team do the driving, Dan. That's what makes the tandem jumping in our roles even more exciting. And there might be several more things that you will uncover. Replacing an entire assembly line is not the same as a 20-minute tandem flight, but I know that if someone can do it, it is my dearest friend Daniel,' said John as he patted Daniel.

It is widely accepted that the demands on modern-day leadership are constantly growing and stress-testing the emotional ability of the individual as a leader. Continuously delivering to the demands without overrunning the budget, keeping the team motivated, giving time to partners, translating executive expectations to executable guidelines for the team, getting the work done with high quality, complying to security/other standards, forecasting business need, preparing the needed talent, constant upskilling, sustaining innovation, contributing to or defining organizational strategy and so on are subsets of expectations on a mid-level manager in most organizations today. And added to these, there would be demands contextual to the line of business which one operates in.

Good leaders overcome the 'leadership challenge' by leaning on their greatest asset—'their teams'. And the ability of a leader to expand the boundary of this 'team' defines how successful and joyful the leader gets to be.

CLEARING AWAY THE BOULDERS

One of the major hurdles in the workplace is to ensure that work flows smoothly and doesn't hit a bottleneck. These could be administrative or logistical issues, compliance issues, people unwilling to cooperate or something else. In fact, this problem is a bigger one than finding the needed talent to get the job done. *Having a highly talented team is not enough if they tend to get stuck constantly with organizational problems which they cannot solve. Especially if the problems have no direct bearing on the delivery at hand, then the team gets even more disinterested to tackle them. This is a key role of leadership—to clear away the boulders and let the team continue to work uninterrupted.*

But do leaders have all the answers all the time and if they don't, how can they drive conviction in their teams?

LEADER AS THE CHIEF VISIONARY OFFICER

The auditorium was filled with over 150 dignitaries from various European companies: heads of technology, CXOs, business unit heads and so on. Ananth Krishnan, Executive Vice-President and Chief Technology Officer of TCS, was one of the keynote speakers speaking on the subject of 'how he drives Innovation within TCS'. One of the questions raised by a dignitary in the audience was 'The biggest challenge we have today is the problem of choice offered by technology—there is a plethora of possibilities in the technology space and it is difficult to know the right area to invest in and explore. As a CTO of TCS, how do you know where to put your bets on? How do you drive your teams with conviction?'

This was the response from Ananth which received a thunderous applause: 'I don't know the answer, although I have a vision as to which direction I should drive my team to. It is very difficult to predict exactly which will be the next big idea that will take off. And so, what I do is to approach it with an attitude of continuous experimentation. Start 100 different threads and filter the ones which show promise to further invest on. Being open with the team, working along with them and making them part of this journey drive conviction.'

During his talk, Ananth also displayed what he calls the 'periodic table of innovation' and explained his belief that 'innovation happens at intersections'. 'Interspersing the diverse technologies and applying lateral thinking provide good clues/starting points for further innovation. More than anything else, you trust your team. They are your biggest bet,' he added with a smile.

Helping the team craft their own adventure and draft their experiences is another selfless trait of leadership. Sometimes you hand over a map, and sometimes just a compass, but what is more important is giving them your trust and confidence that they have what it takes to make the journey, and that you are close by to ensure that they do not get lost. The bigger the adventure, more memorable the experience.

Here is a recollection from a study that we were to conduct for a customer which was considered impractical and borderline crazy. However, getting this right would mean moving the needle forward and changing the perspective of running the business of that domain. We gathered the needed SMEs who were not all convinced with the assignment we signed up for but reluctantly came together. I was discussing with my manager on the need for finding a strong programme manager and how pivotal that role was to get this right. As I narrated the 15 different things which could go wrong, and potential paths we could take to start off, he patiently listened to all of it and said, 'I don't think we can find anyone from outside who understands so much in such a short time and could lead this study. If anyone can do it, it is you! I know you have other things on your plate, let's figure out how to manage together, but this will be a great experience for you and us if we get this right.'

'But there are chances that we might fail and end up looking bad internally as well as with our customers; I have not done this before!' I complained. 'Don't worry about that, let us take it one week at a time, and I will shield you from both sides. Focus on the activities of the week and be clear with your reporting,' he encouraged.

And so it was, we drove the study week by week and faced multiple challenges, the biggest of which was lack of cooperation/conviction from the customer stakeholders and unwillingness to provide information. After a bumpy start, we made slow progress, and every report from my side went out with my role as 'acting programme manager'. We would have a weekly retrospect going through all the activities, data collected, analysis and work on the plan for the next week. 'This is fantastic, I never believed we would come this far; I knew that if someone could do this, it is you!' would be the remark from my manager, week after week apart from other suggestions on what else we could do. The study was delivered within the timeline and was a very useful one for the customers and elevated the level of partnership/business with us.

This was not just a memorable experience for me, but also one of the examples of 'leadership with trust' and willingness to take a risk when there is conviction on the purpose.

GIVE THE STEERING WHEEL

Here is a common experience I am sure some of us would have gone through, but which I believe is a critical leadership trait in interacting with the teams and driving them forward. Several years ago, I was to appear for a driving test in Canada and went to a driving instructor. He was known to be meticulous with his instruction and given that I did not have a lot of driving experience prior to this, I thought this was the teacher to go to. I had a nightmarish three weeks of learning. By the end of the first week, I was beginning to dread the driving lessons and was trying to come up with ideas to skip a class. He was just too strict and too cautious in his approach, not even letting go of the steering wheel fully. This was his way of instruction, 'Bad posture! Stop! Stop! What were you doing? Don't hold the wheel so tight. You didn't look at the mirror in the last 5 minutes. You are not improving with your parking…' and so on. And by the end of three weeks of working with him, my confidence was at an all-time low and I failed the driving test. When I went to him with my marking sheet, he quickly scanned it and said, 'Yes, see,

I told you, you were bad with this, this and this … it's okay, we will try again next time.' I gave him my thanks and after some more exploration found another instructor.

Just a look at his body language was very comforting. He sat with folded hands and cross legged in a relaxed manner and said, 'Let's go for a ride, start the car, just go around your apartment and come back to this place.' I could connect with him in the first 10 minutes of the interaction. He would sit calmly, observe and constantly encourage, 'Well done! Didn't feel a thing, that was a smooth turn, you have a good sense of control….' And at the end of the drive, he would make me pull over after a bit of driving and share some observations on what I could improve. 'Think of this as team work with the other drivers, and play your part, they will reciprocate,' he would say. I cleared the exam.

Of course, there are different styles of coaching (or leadership), and this is not to judge someone to be superior/inferior to the other. It is important to know which style works with which individual of the team and let them get an experience of their own steering wheel.

#GameofDrones

- I am not clear of my goals as a leader; I usually work based on short-term targets which my team cannot relate to sometimes.
- My targets are linked with my boss and his targets with his boss, and I usually push the same to my next level without explaining them the big picture.
- I am worried that my team thinks I don't have as much knowledge as they do.
- I am just the coordinator of the work done by various individuals of the team and take care of the logistics.

- I am not very transparent with my team and withhold information from them.
- I constantly assign tasks to the team to show them that I am in control.
- I don't keep my promises with the team, and if they are interested in something, they follow up with me.
- I am aware of the deficiencies of the team members, rather than their strengths.
- I would like to command respect, rather than earn it; there is no time for such things.
- I believe that being a leader makes me a better human being and I am wiser than everyone in my team.
- I have very high expectations on the team and did not yet find someone who I could groom in the leadership roles.

Now discover and evaluate each roadblock. Think of it as a real drone and see how it is doing. Be honest and review how well you are flying it.

☐ **Fully autonomous flight**

☐ **Guided flights**

☐ **Irregular flight path**

☐ **Unwilling to take off**

#KeyResonatingActions

- Create multiple opportunities for informal interactions.
- Let the team know of your professional or personal accomplishments, beliefs and values that you stand for.

- Share the constraints (under which the team is supposed to deliver) and encourage the team to share their inputs.
- Be very respectful and appreciative of the time of the (individuals of the) team.
- Be a learner, and use every interaction with the team to constantly learn about them.
- Get behind the team during times of appreciation and be ahead of them during times of distress or escalations.
- Share the organizational expectations and plans ahead of the time so that the team knows what to expect when.
- Make it a practice to talk about the value system of the organization, and highlight those who practise good values. Associates tend to follow leaders with a strong display of values.
- Help associates constantly appreciate the value they bring to work and how much the organization benefits from it.
- Create success stories contextual to the team and talk about it, especially with new joiners.

#StickyNoteWorthy

If you want to build a ship, don't drum up people together to collect wood and don't assign them tasks and work, but rather teach them to long for the endless immensity of the sea.

Antoine de Saint-Exupéry

Leadership at any level offers a noble opportunity to grow as an individual by making others successful. Constantly practising to see farther than the others (in the team) even under tough situations and egging the team to live for a collective goal (which is higher than the individual goals) are not just professional callings but life-changing experiences of self-learning. When the team recognizes the selfless positive drive of their leader, they do not fail to reciprocate, and such teams celebrate constant and often fulfilling successes marked by joyful experiences every day.

17

DIVE AND RETURN

This story takes place at a time when sea exploration was done on traditional sailing ships driven by the rowing power of men assisted by wind, driving the huge sails. Merchandise via sea was common, although risk prone. Most ships made it to the destination, but some unlucky ones went down to permanently lie with the ocean bed until they were found years later, accidentally that is!

And treasure diving as a profession quickly gained popularity. Sea diving to find natural pearls and corals was an established profession already, and there were accidental discoveries of sunken ships which were pushed closer to the shoreline by the sea.

Rich merchants constantly looked out for deep sea expert divers who could fetch them the riches lost beneath the majestic waters apart from pearls. This was not an easy job, and the divers were picked up after rigorous tests. The exploration for riches was driven more by hope and excitement of discovery than certainty. Not many succeeded with these missions and returned empty-handed. Some divers never surfaced back. One merchant was particularly successful in this trexploration (as they called it in short for treasure exploration), and although his real name was not so popular, his successes made him come to be known as Mr Trex in all the lands and over the seas.

Trex knew how to find the right divers and he conducted some tricky tests before he picked up a new diver into the team. He would test the ability of the divers to stay under water for a long time and how well they worked with each other. He would look for those who could 'see beneath the surface' as he called it. Although he had a good number of them, he had the knack of understanding if a specific set of divers were suited to the task at hand. And given the nature of the new lead he was after, he needed another expert diver to lead the team.

Trex announced this in the towns and cities where he found good divers and in those rare areas where he suspected lived some of the great yet undiscovered divers. Many divers responded to his invitation to be part of his team, 50 of them to be precise, whereas on this occasion he just needed one.

The test was to be done in a location slightly inwards into the sea, where there was a hidden ocean ridge. There was a rift between the rocks below, which was deep enough to test any expert diver. This was also contained so perfectly between the hills underneath that this resembled a lake formation underneath the sea. Trex being himself an expert diver of his time found this spot accidentally in one of his adventures. He decided to use this environment for the test.

The date for the test was fixed, and all the divers were asked to prepare. Among the 50 divers, 20 approached Trex's team to understand the environment. The rest 30 came directly to the test and were eliminated without even letting them take the test. 'First failure lies in not being curious about your playground. That is essential for preparation,' Trex told the others.

A rope which measured roughly 1,000 feet distance of able-bodied men was prepared. And the diver who could take the most part of the rope into the rift would be adjudged the winner. 'You could find some unpleasant surprises in there; from this point onwards, you are responsible for what happens to you,' said Trex as the divers took turns one by one to jump. Some took caution and left the place.

The first few went as deep as 200 feet and came back to the surface. 'It is pitch dark; the light is blocked by the ridges; it is impossible to see and no one knows what is coming at you; this is an impossible test,' they said. 'We shall see,' replied Trex. A few more took the rope deeper than 250 feet and were certain that this would be the farthest that anyone could make it. 'I almost got killed; I either hit a sea creature or the rock of the ridge, I can't tell. No one can go deeper,' one diver said.

While the other divers continued to test their mettle, there were three shabby looking divers who remained silent and waited their turn. No one interacted with them as they thought these were goons trying to grab a meal with a fake exhibition of their non-existent skill (Trex usually offered food for the day for all those who participated). Trex noticed them before but did not pay much attention. 'I hope these lads don't kill themselves for the lure of a meal,' he thought.

As the other divers finished, Trex motioned one of them to go next. 'But, sir, we do it together. Andy here will lead the dive and we will work with him in a line underwater tugging on to the rope and lowering him as he goes to the ocean floor,' said a man who called himself Tim. Andy was looking at the ground smiling. 'Andy is good, sir; he doesn't fear water and darkness,' said Murphy who looked short and resembled a walking dolphin. 'No one spoke about touching the floor; we don't know how deep the rift is; you will go as deep as the rope would take you and come back before you die in there. I don't want your death on my conscience,' said Trex authoritatively. 'Don't worry, sir, we will do so. We grew up all our life at sea and we don't fear it. Andy here can see beneath the sea better than on land,' said Tim and Trex noticed that Andy was blind.

The three men prepared to dive. Andy asked Tim and Murphy to find a heavy rock and tie it to one end of the rope.

He took the rock, holding tightly to the knot and jumped off the vessel into the rift and after him the rope went in like a snap. Tim held on to it and jumped right behind. Murphy followed shortly after and before he did, 'When we give a signal, pull us back up; *we rely on our courage to go in and support of our friends to pull us out,*' he said. Trex let out a whistle in appreciation. 'We will pull you back up, lads; I will dive myself in to save the best team I have ever found,' he said as the other divers nodded in agreement.

As Trex and the other divers watched in amazement, the rope went quickly in by 800 feet in a span of few moments. And after a while, as the rope hit 900 feet, there a momentary pause and a strong tug was felt. 'This is the signal; the rock has been loosened; pull the divers up,' yelled Trex and the rest of the divers put their might into hoisting the three brave divers out.

Andy came last and he was still smiling. 'My uncle said I was washed ashore as a kid and was raised by the whales,' he said. 'I never believed it, but I feel at home under water. Diving, in our tribe, is as much cooperation as it is courage and without your support the return is not possible,' he concluded as he picked up a small sack which he found at the bottom of the rift.

'You are in, all three of you. I sunk this sack of pearls at this place a long time ago and did not believe someone would go as deep to recover it back. *The measuring rope was a distraction. The real test was in picking up what you dived in for!*' said Trex. 'Andy, you will lead the diving exploration, and your eyes Tim and Murphy will follow you along with the other divers,' concluded Trex as the others on board applauded the three.

#WorkplaceWhispers

'Deliver on commitment' and 'commit to deliver' are two common battle cries at the competitive workplace today. Unless

you are a single person workforce (now I am being dramatic on purpose!),

- you must often find yourself making commitments based on someone (a team) or something (an operating structure) or
- you must be working hard to deliver to the commitments made by someone else (and not let them lose their face).

The sales teams make the dive, banking on the delivery teams to hold the line and keep up the promise. The onshore or the on-field teams make the dive, banking on the offshore or back-end support teams holding the line. And so on. While this interdependence is structural, most times, sensation happens when someone makes an impossible dive backed by an extraordinary team. And we see this often too.

When an executive takes stage launching a new product or demonstrating a new capability to thousands of prospects, he is banking on a huge back haul, holding his line and ensuring that he doesn't lose his face. This is much more than team work, this is trust at the highest level. And a critical aspect of this is having a firm and common view of the end goal. Let us examine three diverse perspectives based on the story (I encourage you to draw more).

THE ROPE SHOULD NOT SNAP: IMPORTANCE OF KNOWING THE ENVIRONMENT

The importance of preparation and contextual knowledge of the environment cannot be underrated. Most failures on stage (or promises of delivery) happen due to miscalculation/misunderstanding of the environmental forces (organizational context). Often we see exuberant salespeople talking of how great their product/service is, without putting any effort to understand the context where it will operate. If you have been on the receiving end of such promises from someone without knowing what you really need or your current situation, then you know how it feels.

Then there are others too who start with knowing you/your context, do their homework and come back to make a pitch which connects with you. Same goes with making demonstrations and presentations too. Preparation is paramount—simulating failures, rehearsing, pre-empting questions, having enough data points—all of these ensure that the rope doesn't snap when you dive in. Having said that...

THE MEASURING ROPE IS A DISTRACTION

With a strong grounding in QA for several years, I can say with conviction that measures are not just important, but right measures (and the associated metrics) are crucial for continuous improvements. Having said that, one should *not lose sight of the end goal* while being compliant to measures.

Prabhu is the head of operations for a company which supplies raw material to a furniture manufacturer. He has monthly reviews with his team to check the health of the metrics and how they are coping with the commitments. After the initial few minutes of reviewing the metrics, he would ask, 'Now let us understand something that the metrics wouldn't tell me: What are customers saying? Do we understand their commitments and their plans? How has been the customer experience? What more can we do creatively to gather their feedback? Did any of you make a field visit to get first-hand input from the end customers? I have met the production line manager of our customer yesterday, and while our metrics are looking good, our customers are not too happy. I would like to add a subjective metric of "customer happiness index"; let us discuss on how to measure this smartly and review it together.'

Getting the metrics and measures right will not be useful if the end goal is forgotten.

'BOLD ENOUGH TO DIVE'

Even when the organization has a great team (self or from suppliers), rigorous preparation and great ideas, it would still need sponsorship of a leader with right experience to sense the merit of the idea, trust on the team and courage to make the dive. In Mobile World Congress 2018 at Barcelona, I witnessed a senior executive make a flawless demonstration of a cutting-edge feature on stage to his customers and partners. I appreciated him for the good show and asked him as to how he delivers these presentations with such ease and boldness. He said, 'I know my team and how much preparation and hard work they put in each time. It is a team that does not let me fail, it never did so far. I trust them with my life on stage.'

#GameofDrones

AS AN INDIVIDUAL

- I have no idea why certain measures and metrics are in place or why I get constant reminders on compliance.
- I am usually happy when I meet my numbers and stand green on the reports.
- I am cut off from the big picture and my lead manages everything I do. I am fine with that.
- I don't spend time knowing the customer asks or problems and dive right into new projects. All I need to know are deadlines.
- There are no visible measures of progress in my team, as we are working on never-been-done-before innovative products. We work based on intuition and take chances.

- I think I am working on something phenomenal, but I expect the organization to automatically take note of this. I do not put effort to explain the relevance of what I am working on or the support I provide.

AS A LEADER

- I do not fully understand and appreciate the support structure which is helping me take the lead.
- I do not spend time appreciating the back office teams or the supplier organization for the continuous success which they deliver to me.
- I seldom take time explaining the business context and the value being delivered by us to the teams.
- I want my teams to do more so that I can dive further, but I do not have a way to translate this ask in a way that they can understand and execute.

Now discover and evaluate each roadblock. Think of it as a real drone and see how it is doing. Be honest and review how well you are flying it.

- ☐ **Fully autonomous flight**
- ☐ **Guided flights**
- ☐ **Irregular flight path**
- ☐ **Unwilling to take off**

#KeyResonatingActions

AS AN INDIVIDUAL

- Seek help to understand the big picture—what really is the problem being solved and what is driving the operating model (why are you structured the way you are).

- Discuss the measures employed in the workplace and their connection to the end goal.
- When there is an expectation (of information or service from you), seek clarifications on how your inputs will be processed and who will be benefited.
- Share feedback (and be open to feedback as well), if you see that the measures are not aligned to the end goal(s).
- Express enthusiasm visibly. It not only motivates the management (or the people diving in) but also others in the team.
- Share the importance of your work to others openly and solicit the same. Understanding each other's perspective of value delivered goes a long way in strengthening the 'line'.

AS A LEADER

- Appreciate often and share timely feedback, especially after each 'dive' (meeting, presentation, demo, sales pitch and so on).
- Focus on training and building other divers (building leadership).
- Generate enthusiasm end to end. A bored team cannot help generating sensational dives. And it is not enough to motivate a team in isolation, but everyone that is lined up in an end goal, either directly or indirectly (support teams which are usually invisible), including customers.

#StickyNoteWorthy

It's not what you achieve, it's what you overcome. That's what defines your career.

Carlton Fisk

A marked characteristic of a resilient organization which remains unshaken to external forces is having teams that watch each other's back with unbroken trust, encourage each other to overcome challenges and constantly dive deeper with enthusiasm.

18

IF ALL YOU CAN IS DIG

Several hundred years ago, in ancient India lived a sculptor by name Giri in the kingdom of Vinama. Vinama was a thriving kingdom in between the Vindhya hills. There was a lot of respect for arts and literature, which were treated as divine gifts for those who practised them.

Giri worked in the king's palace and was known for his artful sculptures carved out of stone. He worked very hard and created several masterpieces for the palace. He attributed his special skills to his lineage. 'We have been in the art of sculpting for countless generations, with each generation better than the previous one. I am sure my son will be better than me,' he used to proudly announce to his relatives and royal staff.

Giri lived a comfortable life in a humble home close to the palace like all the others who worked in the palace did. The king and the royal members had special interest in art, and Giri was rewarded with several gifts and felicitations very often.

And as destiny would have it, Giri's son Surang fancied the tools of the trade as a kid. He played with hammer and chisel, much to the delight of his father. 'My son will create eternal masterpieces,' he told himself. But strangely, Surang spent time piercing stone and digging the ground. 'A playful artist, very soon the meaning will emerge,' an impatient Giri told himself.

'Oh, he is just a kid, give him time,' his wife and his friends told him.

One day as Surang was playing in the house yard, the chief royal architect passed by. He paused in front of the house, observed the kid for a while and announced loudly, 'This kid will become one of the greatest artists of the land, such poise and control at such a young age!' Giri was watching with happiness brimming all over his face. He said, 'O, great one! Does that mean he will be the best sculptor the world has ever seen?' 'His work will be priceless and will stand the test of time; he will build something which no one else did before,' the architect said and left the place. Giri proudly spread the word to all his friends and colleagues at the palace.

As years passed by, Giri intently waited for his son to create marvels in sculpting. But to his dismay, his son only showed interest in digging the ground and boring hollows in rock. As he grew older, he brought a variety of shovels, spades and other heavy metals he could find and dug. 'Are you testing the quality of the stone, son?' Giri would ask. 'No, father, I like to dig deep into the earth and continue digging. I am driven towards it,' replied Surang.

'Maybe you should come back to reality and start his education and teach him other arts,' advised his friends. 'I tried that,' cried Giri in utter sadness. 'Nothing interests Surang more than digging. His teacher told me in no sweeter words that he has not seen an idiot who can parallel his dumbness in formal education. Oh! This is shameful. At this age I had already created several sculptures in my time. And I thought my son would be a child prodigy,' he said. 'Don't give up so soon; he is still so young; try other teachers and different arts,' his friends encouraged him.

But try as hard as he could, Giri failed in finding a single avocation or subject where Surang showed interest or aptitude. He just liked to dig. 'Don't you have any interest towards moulding the rocks? We have been sculpting for generations.

I thought your fascination for mud is to make a new form of sculpture. It doesn't seem to be so.'

'No, father, it is not mud, but making a perfect path into the earth that I am fascinated about,' said Surang. 'Are you the son of a rat?!' yelled Giri and left the place. To please his father, Surang tried hard at learning other subjects, but he did not have the aptitude for it and quickly lost interest. 'It is pointless, nothing but the metal and drilling away paths through hard obstructions interests me. I must be having no future in this world,' thought Surang.

Several more years passed, and despite the rebuke of his family, friends and society at large, Surang did not leave his calling. Although he was born in a high-class family, he went to work with the workers of the land who helped build pathways for the kingdom. He was called to help create paths which were impossible to make through the Vindhya hills. 'He knows exactly where to crack open the path at its weakest, without collapsing the structure,' his co-workers praised him. Whilst Surang found peace doing what he did, his heart ached for the fact that he could not bring joy to his father. 'Son of a great lineage of sculptors, working to build pathways with working class, what a great misfortune!' said everyone.

One day, the architect who foretold Surang's future passed by Giri's house. Furious, Giri rushed to him and demanded, 'You foretold greatness for my son. All he cares about is digging the ground and nothing else. He has learnt nothing else. How can he create a work of art? Because of you I have lost my face in front of everyone,' he cried.

The chief architect calmly replied with a smile, 'Call for your son.' As Surang approached, he asked, 'What do you most care about?' 'I love to go deep into the earth; I love to create pathways into the heart of the planet. I dream of ways underground that can last forever,' said Surang. '*If all you can is dig, then dig so well that the pathways you create amaze the creator. Leave all doubt and despair.* Your work will ensue a new art into the world and will ensure that this land has a future,' he said and left, leaving Giri astonished and infuriated. 'So the royal architect is not wise after all. Who can make anything out of digging?' he said.

Word spread to the chief minister of the kingdom about the unique skill possessed by Surang. 'I would like to speak to your son, Giri, please call for him,' said Neela. 'He is fit for nothing, sir, but I will do as you have ordered,' said Giri and sent Surang to meet the chief minister of the kingdom, Neela.

'Did you not attempt to learn anything else? Your family served this kingdom for several generations and you are the first one that is an exception. And it troubles me to see your father so sad,' Neela asked Surang.

'Sir! I have dug deep within myself too as much as I have in the ground. Nothing other than digging inspires me. I have nothing else to give, nor feel ashamed of. I am at peace with this fact. I accept my misfortune of not being of service to the king,' replied Surang respectfully.

'On the contrary, I have seen some of the pathways you have helped creating, very impressive. The chief architect also has a high regard for you. I have a vision which I think only you can fulfil, but it will take some more structured training for you to augment your unique skill and you can be of great service to the king,' Neela said.

'I am afraid, my faculties do not permit me to learn anything else that doesn't involve digging, sir. What do you wish to teach me?' Surang asked.

'I will not teach you anything new, you will work with the engineers of the palace and begin the work of your life,' Neela smiled. 'I will only bring you in if you swear an oath of secrecy—this will remain a secret for life. Are you willing to take this on *to put your passion to greater good, with no glory coming your way?*' asked Neela enquiringly. 'I will, sir. If there is meaning and purpose to my passion, I seek no further glory than this, *even if it consumes the rest of my life, I will dig,'* Surang's enthusiasm was contagious. 'Son! I could even think of this vision because I knew I could rely on you and no one else. You will create a pathway from the heart of the palace through the Vindhya mountains, which would open on the far side. Whenever adversity strikes on the palace, this passage will ensure safety and security of the royal family and future for the kingdom for a long time. I will tell your father that you have joined my guard in the palace; all that digging has made you strong after all,' said Neela.

Surang spent the next 30 years working on the passage along with the most trusted engineers of the kingdom, some of whom lost their lives during the process. It is said that the passage lasted several hundred years and have saved the lives of the royal families which ruled the land generations after generations. The passage and its creator have been kept as a secret only passed down from one king to the other. While Surang did not gain any recognition during his time, he built something remarkable just doing what he did, so well. To the last day he remembered the words of the wise man, *'If all you can do is dig, then dig so well that the pathways you create amaze the creator!'*

This ushered in a new art into the world as foretold by the wise man. Ever since, it has become common to create hidden passageways around palaces of the kingdoms and using underground pathways to divert flow of streams to bring water to the cities.

#WorkplaceWhispers

Like most associates in their formative years in an organization, I intended to find out that one (or two) skill which would safeguard my future and help me make it big in the company. Is it programming language proficiency or doing lot of certifications or getting into a project which was working on cutting-edge stuff or something else? This led me into spending several hours reading up on the Internet on which technology was better than the other, which certification to crack early on and get ahead in the line.

I used to interact with multiple SMEs in the organization to know their opinions and it left me more confused than ever. Not having a computer science background in my college made me feel insecure and have a low self-esteem in front of my colleagues with better technical know-how. I used to pick up a line of learning, spend a few days/weeks before hitting upon something else and hop on to it. This continued for well over couple of years, with a side effect of gaining a lot of generalist knowledge in technology (which would prove useful several years later).

EXPERT ADVICE

In one of those determined searches, I hit upon some (open source) forums where gurus in that specific technology would participate and provide answers to the questions posed by young and proficient developers. And there was a consistent piece of advice from such experts which I have paraphrased as follows: 'It doesn't matter which line of learning (which technology) you choose to dabble on, as long as it appeals to you. Gaining expertise is a matter of persistence and pain (efforts). And one would be willing to take on that pain if there is satisfaction and fulfilment in it.'

LEARNING TO LEARN

This is a common observation interacting with successful individuals from different companies and backgrounds—most of them had started with modest backgrounds in their respective organizations, but in a few years' time, with their focus and determination, ended up with very good roles and important projects in their companies. For most of them it was unimaginable to dream up their current work/role when they got started. 'I'd never imagined I will be getting into something like this from where I started,' they would say. And in almost all the cases, the clue to this progression was their ability to stay focused on what they were into and gain in-depth understanding of the subject without getting distracted. They were practising one thing well—'learning to learn'.

'BUT I AM DISTRACTED'

While this might sound counterintuitive, one of the inhibitors to learning is *distraction due to contrast and comparison*. Associates come to me asking for advice and help to move them into another area. When I ask them for feedback on what is wrong with the area they are working on, and if they have extracted all the learning possible, they would say, 'That other area looks way cooler than mine, more visibility.' While this is not a right or wrong discussion (it is perfectly okay to be trying different things), one should be mindful about the choices and be persistent with learning.

PICK THE FIELD THAT OFFERS JOYFUL PAIN

One good thing about a modern workplace (perhaps it has always been the case when one looks closely) is that it promotes diversity of skills. Every associate, as long as there is willingness to fully apply oneself, is precious in the organization. While a good approach which the young professionals could take is to persist with learning and try to gain expertise in one area before hopping on to the other, there is a big need for multifaceted associates as well with a broad understanding of their domain. And again this is not a 'which-line-of-work-is-easier-than-the-other' discussion or which path gives easy progress. It is more about one's inclination, and in which field of work one is willing to take on 'joyful pain' as a means to develop expertise.

AS AN INDIVIDUAL

- I am constantly restless at work; I feel that other colleagues are doing more interesting stuff.
- I get demotivated by people constantly posting news about new certifications and trainings.
- I crave for visibility, does not matter what job role I perform.
- I do not fully understand the opportunity offered by my current field of work.
- I feel that the organization is forcibly keeping me in this place; I deserve better opportunities for the person that I am.
- My other friends have quit the organization or doing good work in different locations; I feel stuck here.
- I see that only few associates are favoured by my team management; only they are getting repeated opportunities.

AS A LEADER

- I have many groups in my portfolio, but clearly I tend to be preferential to few of those over the others.
- I keep my interactions limited to a few performing individuals only in my areas of interest.
- I have strong opinions about who should do what and not flexible to move associates around; it might disturb our deliverables to customers.

Now discover and evaluate each roadblock. Think of it as a real drone and see how it is doing. Be honest and review how well you are flying it.

- ☐ **Fully autonomous flight**
- ☐ **Guided flights**
- ☐ **Irregular flight path**
- ☐ **Unwilling to take off**

#KeyResonatingActions

AS AN INDIVIDUAL

- Be proud to be doing what you are doing (in case you enjoy what you do); this is a great way to succeed (while being open to learning).
- Take constant feedback or mentoring sessions to understand your domain better and constantly add complementary skills which can enrich your learning.
- If you have completely mastered the current field of work (no more joyful pain), look for a different field which could provide the same.
- Validate your interest in a different field (than your own) by trying to learn about the 'day in the life' of an associate working in that field—both the positives and the hardships involved.
    - o Make subjective and objective assessments based on these inputs if the switch is something that you will enjoy.
- Work on a transition plan before you approach management asking for a change—prepare another associate who could take over from you/ask for support from management to enable this.
- Before giving up on a field (to hop to another one), thoroughly evaluate the opportunity and the field of work

by discussing with someone who loves (usually an SME) this field.

AS A LEADER

- In general, encourage change in the field of work for the associates (subject to the work context and opportunity). This will motivate the team and allow grooming of associates with multiple skills.
- Create forums where skilled associates can talk about their area of work and explain the journey involved to gain expertise (learning paths).
- Encourage specialist groups where one SME can be put together with the others on a learning path.
- Exhibit visible tolerance to skill diversity and respect associates with different skills and skill levels.

#StickyNoteWorthy

An expert is a man who has made all the mistakes which can be made in a very narrow field.

Niels Bohr

The story of Surang is inspired by individuals who take genuine pride in what they want to do and are not swayed by public opinion of what is right or wrong for them. Such individuals spend selfless time to create works of immense value, and not even wait for appreciation. This requires one to be true to oneself and experiment with (*keep digging into*) several activities/ projects before one could really understand what work makes one's heart truly jump with joy, often requiring making several mistakes along the way as a means to learn more.

19

THE SPRING, THE CAVE AND THE LITTLE GIRL

The village of Grainhinge had the most fertile lands of the kingdom. They generated so much yield that it was enough to feed the rest of the kingdom, and the crops provided this bounty all year round. The lands of Grainhinge were fed by the stream originating from a nearby hill in the forest, and there was a belief that this stream carried rich minerals and nutrients to the lands, which led to the magical yield round the year. The villagers did not worry about the monsoon, and as if by coordinated destiny, the seasons were always favourable to Grainhinge.

No one knew the source of this stream. The stream gushed out from what looked like the mouth of a hill on one side of the village and was covered by dense forest all around it. The villagers didn't much care and were thankful for this bounty. They worked together on all the lands and ensured that utmost care was given to each and every crop, and more importantly, they ensured that the water from the stream was not wasted. The villagers cared about the lands and the noble purpose that they were serving—'feeding the kingdom'. Also the water from the stream flowed to the village only for few days in a year. But when well directed, it was enough to make fertile the entire lands of the village.

As this continued for several generations, the wisdom was passed on from one generation to the other, and the people of the kingdom were happy.

Blame it on fate or collective failure, as the village and the kingdom continued to flourish, people *got lost in the plenty they had and stopped talking about what was the reason for this abundance.* The king sent a lot of gifts to the village as the previous kings did, but earlier those gifts were shared, not just in the village but to the neighbouring ones too. Many farmers got together to work on these lands foregoing their own, and why shouldn't they? They worked together as one big family. No one staked a claim saying, 'this is mine' and 'that is yours'. This helped them utilize the stream also well. But then slowly the a*ppreciation* and *the state of doing-so-well took over their heads.* People *started claiming the rewards and steered away from what they loved doing, their purpose*—'providing food for the kingdom'.

'No one really knew why it happened or what caused the stream to stop, but my great grandfather told me this when he was lying on his deathbed,' said Grandpa Sam, who was himself quite old and told stories to the children in the village square.

'There was an interdependence that the villagers missed. We worked together and for each other; we worked because we loved to do so and the stream drew inspiration from us. We depended on it, and it knew that we used it well for a larger good. Then there were couple of years when the stream was neglected. The elders of the village told the middlemen, and they told someone else to water the lands, but no one had the time to do so. There was so much to enjoy. "We have so much; it doesn't matter if we stop agriculture this year; we have enough to survive generations," they told each other and spent time in festivities … and this continued for five years. The supplies started to go down and when the king placed a huge order, the elders of the village realized their mistake! It was too late by then. The younger lads overseeing the lands told the elders that the stream stopped coming through for two years and although the yield was good, the lands lost their fertility, and they were not producing enough.

"Then why didn't you alert us!" demanded the elders of the village. "We didn't know that we should; no one told us what happens when; we just assumed this is how it is supposed to be and we did our best to irrigate. When the stream didn't come through, we used water from the river close by," they replied angrily.

What followed was a mad rush to safeguard what was left—control over the lands, over the grain, over the name and rewards and competition between farmers started. The other villagers who used to come together parted ways. They didn't want a share of the blame, "We offered to help, but it is your problem now; we will get back to tending our lands...." The King was furious, and he punished the elders of the village, but that didn't solve the problem and the situation deteriorated over time,' Grandpa Sam recollected his great grandfather's story.

'My great grandfather also told us something more valuable,' he said, 'May be our biggest mistake was *we stopped telling stories of good times and what made us good. Remembering your roots and good practices which have made you what you are is so important.* We stopped doing that, and we forgot deep down our interdependence with the stream and that's why I ensure that you know the story of our village,' Grandpa Sam tried to conclude with a sigh. 'But that's not it! You never tell us about what happened to the stream and to the hill, and did no one try to see where the stream went?' Peter, a village lad, demanded. 'Enough!' boomed George, Peter's father. 'You do not have enough age to hear horror stories yet, get back to your homes, it is time for bed,' he told the disappointed kids. 'Don't be so hard on them, George, you did the same when you were a kid, you wanted to know more...,' smiled Grandpa Sam. 'And you didn't tell me, until I came of age! Rest now, old Sam,' George headed back to his home.

There were only a few in the village who knew the story of the stream. And no one spoke about it for the fear of bad consequences which may follow. It was discussed in hushed tones that the place where the stream originated, 'the mouth of the hill', as Grandpa Sam put it, was caved in. It turned out to be a scary dark cave with a labyrinth which led nowhere. Many brave villagers and strong soldiers from the king's army ventured into the cave and never returned. Only one soldier came back to tell the story, but he died soon after. 'It is pitch dark, and the torches go out as soon as you enter. It is as if the cave is testing you. It asked me to choose "left or right", and I chose to get out instead. I did not go deep enough so could run back out of the cave, but almost lost my life. There are creepy things on the ground and horrifying noises; no man can make it in and get out alive!' the soldier seemed to have narrated to his fellowmen. The king ordered a perimeter to be set up around the cave with rocks, fallen trees and other natural obstructions, and Grainhinge was moved farther away. In several years, the forest consumed what used to be the old dwelling of Grainhinge, and the cave was lost in the forest.

The soldier who made it out and died went delirious and repeated this song on his death bed:

Right or left, you make a choice
will kill you now, if I see in you a vice
you will hit a lure or two in my labyrinth
or consumed by fear, will smash you to my plinth....

The solider hailed from Grainhinge, and his story passed down to his son and to the next one. Grandpa Sam and old Joe (grandson of the soldier), who died recently, were friends and Joe passed on this story to Sam. Joe had a daughter who married a blacksmith of the village, and they had a baby girl Cecilia who was born blind. Cecilia however was gifted with a beautiful voice, and her mamma told her friends, 'Even when she cries, it feels like a song….'

Little Ceci as she was called in the village was a pretty girl, and everyone took care of her. She was the apple of the eye of the village, and her songs brought the village together. 'You will soon overtake my position at the square and attention from the kids away from my stories, little one,' Grandpa Sam lovingly told little Ceci, who was now seven years old and beginning to sing folk songs which she learnt from her mother.

Cecilia was also a courageous girl. 'You have your grandfather's courage,' someone from the village commented when Cecilia accidentally held a snake near the village well. To the utter shock of the onlookers, the snake didn't seem to mind it too and played in her hands. 'But her grandfather was a coward; he flew back from the cave,' someone else shouted. 'No, he was not! He did not run, he came back to narrate the story, you fool! Else no one would know what happened in there,' Cecilia's mom yelled back. 'What cave, mamma,' little Ceci asked her mother later in the evening. 'Nothing to worry about, dear, let me teach you a new song,' her mother distracted little Ceci and the matter trailed off.

The kids of the village constantly played in the forest surrounding the village. Little Ceci joined them sometimes and when the kids got tired of playing, they made Ceci sing for them. 'You sing so well, even the squirrels and rabbits come closer to hear you…,' cute Johnny remarked. 'Don't you worry that you can't see?' the innocent one asked Ceci. 'But everybody takes care of me, and I want to sing for all of you, as much as I can; I am happy singing,' Ceci replied. And right she was!

'One thing which united all of us after the good old stream is the little Ceci's singing; I see folks from neighbouring villages visiting us too to listen to her at the village square. And this time they got us some grain from their granaries! Makes me remember old days…,' Grandpa Sam told the villagers. And little Ceci got better and better at singing with each passing day. As she turned 10 that year, her mother permitted her one day to go to the square to listen to Grand Sam's village story. Cecilia listened intently and Grand Sam saw for the first time a sad expression on the child's face. 'Now now, don't worry child, this is a just a story…. Johnny, lead her home, will you?' Grandpa Sam said in a kind voice.

Cecilia was drawn into the story and pleaded with her mother to say more. She also made a song of her own from the story and started singing beautifully.

Story of an old village, glory of the people
…they lived together, worked together
farming was the staple…
la la la la la … la la la la laa laa….

'Oh, sweet child! That is so beautiful; you should sing at the square,' encouraged her mamma when Cecilia finished her song. This became the new attraction and the fame spread quickly to the neighbouring villages.

They were brothers in the same goal, food for the country
…sprightly stream to nourish the land, making food in bounty….

Her song was as magical as the stream and melted the hearts of the villagers. 'This is a signal to us; we should come together again,' they spoke emotionally. 'And work on what; the lands have long gone barren,' shouted another. 'There is no harm trying; we gave up on the stream and it gave up on us, may be the reverse will work too,' George encouraged. 'If nothing else, coming together and sharing what we have will not make our situation worse; I never thought I will live to hear and see this day; Old Joe would be proud of Ceci,' Grandpa Sam spoke with tears welling up in his eyes.

It was easier said than done, but the 'song of Ceci' as it came to be known kept the folks together. The children continued to play in the forest with more friends joining them from neighbouring villages, as their parents started clearing the forgotten lands to start farming again.

And one day, the children wandered off deep into the forest as they were playing hide and seek. Little Ceci was lost but remained cheerful singing her songs. 'Oh, Mr Snake, is that you? Don't worry I am fine…,' she felt a soft, thick rope-like thing crawl on her feet. 'Walk towards me … who dares enter my domain in the night!' boomed a voice which seemed to come from the direction the snake went. 'Who is calling out to me? Are you a forest dweller?' Cecilia shouted back and walked in that direction. As she entered the mouth of the cave which was completely hidden by thick moss, overgrown creepers and roots, she felt a strange smell which she never came across in the forest or in the village. 'What is this place? Where am I?' Cecilia asked. 'You are in my mouth and I will kill you,' boomed a heavy voice as if the rocks were speaking.

'Okay, you sound angry; do you want me to sing for you?' Cecilia offered.

'Ah! So this is a fearless one,' the cave thought. 'I am the cave that your villagers dread! Are you not scared of the dark and the creatures on the ground? They might kill you any instant!' the cave tried to scare Cecilia.

'No, actually, I never saw light in my life Mr Cave, but I hear everything. I think the creatures on the ground are being nice; they are moving away from me and clearing the path…. They have always been nice to me, ever since they heard my song. They want to hear it again perhaps…,' Cecilia replied as the cave resonated with the hissing noises of the snakes on the ground.

'Silence, crawlers! You are no good today, I will kill her myself. So why are you here? Who told you of the treasure I hold? If I see vice in you, I will kill you,' the cave demanded. 'My treasure is my singing and love towards everyone around me; I don't want anything else. You called me in, remember? I lost my way and was waiting for my friends,' Cecilia replied walking carefully not to step on anything on the ground and accidentally cause any hurt.

'No fear, no greed, only love for others!' the cave seemed to moisten a little bit. 'Well then, *right or left, you make a choice, will kill you now, if I see in you a vice,*' the cave threw the puzzle at Cecilia.

'*Right or left is all the same, let's do it together and play the game,*' Cecilia sang sweetly in reply. Even the snakes seem to hiss together in a smile, and there was a distant sound of water gushing from within.

'Alright!' the cave thundered, 'Take the passage to the right and you will find your eyesight there. I think that is what you want to have, you greedy little one!' lured the cave and continued:

'You will hit a lure or two in my labyrinth
or consumed by fear, will smash you to my plinth....'

'My sight is my song, which I spread in glee.... I will sing along, and it will soon touch thee ... lalalala laa laa,' Cecila sang in response.

The cave seemed to soften further as the child embraced *choice with togetherness* and *both fear and lure with kindness*.

'Mr Cave, I have a favourite song which my village seemed to like and they say that this is the best narration of the village story. I will sing it for you and maybe you can help us?' so saying Cecilia started singing the story of the village. As she beautifully sang the story of Grainhinge, how the people went from a state of happiness to a state of utter despair and pain, the walls of the cave started to melt down, the snakes started turning into gentle creepers and the labyrinths collapsed in place.

As Cecilia finished her song, a kind voice which sounded like smooth gushing water which could quench a million thirsts spoke to her, 'Dear child! This cave was the result of *neglect (which lead to darkness), confusion and blame (which formed the labyrinths) and fear and greed (which created the scary creatures).* The village people and this kingdom consumed the magical waters for centuries but showed ingratitude, and their attitude created this curse. You brought them together with your gift of singing, even before you entered this cave. You have made them empathize with their past and made them to come together once again. Their regained spirit and your fearlessness overpowered this cave and *the caves which they created in their hearts…*,' so saying the voice went silent and Cecilia could feel the cold spray of a gushing steam close by.

A gentle creeper clutched Cecilia's hand and led her carefully out to the edge of the forest where a big search party was on, looking for Cecilia. As Cecilia gently strolled out of the forest with the stream following along, the villagers jumped with utter jubilation and a pleasant shock which the sight of the stream ensued. Grandpa Sam hugged Cecilia and bowed to the stream. 'From today at the village square there will be a new story and a new song,' he announced to the villagers who cheered in a loud applause.

#WorkplaceWhispers

The buzz and pulls of the workplace day after day, milestone after milestone, project after project, quarter on quarter and so on keep writing and rewriting on the active memories of the individuals constantly. And it is common experience that while successes, appreciations and good things in general become part of the stride and quickly forgotten, the indigestible stuff—failures, negative aspects, unsolved problems, hurtful remarks and so on—remain as clogs in the gut. Over a period of time, and unless these are flushed out, they result in a team culture which turns heavy and apathetic. Add to this, there is a constant (in most cases) movement of old-timers moving on and newcomers joining into the team. While this brings in fresh energy, it also means that with every associate that the team bids adieu to, some of the good legacy of the past is also lost.

Remembering, cherishing and celebrating the roots, the strengths of the team (or the USP of the company), the value system and all the instances of challenges overcome are not just good to have needs but also essential survival strategies for a team/organization.

A PART OF INITIAL INDUCTION

Along with the initial learning programme which an associate gets to go through especially while joining a new team, it will be useful to interact with the seniors of the team to understand the founding principles/goals, big milestones achieved, some of the key foundational work which went into shaping the team and aspirations. This will enable one to appreciate the foundation on which one is standing on and feel grateful for the work done by others who made the opportunity of today possible. It is an active practice in one of the large programmes that I was part of where the senior leaders take one of the sessions of the initial learning programme to talk about the history, milestones and the culture of the unit (what and why).

THE LEADER AS THE CHIEF STORYTELLER

I was to be interviewed by the head of our segment and a senior leader in the organization, Jayaram Nutulapati, for an onshore leadership role in one of his large accounts. As I waited for him in his cabin, I kept looking at my notes (I was asked to share prior to this meeting my reflections on my key achievements, strengths and what I will bring to the table if selected here), and what should be the most impressive opening lines after I greet him. To my pleasant surprise, the interview turned out to be an enjoyable experience of learning.

Jayaram spent the initial 40 minutes of the 'interview' talking about the nature of work in the business unit and the past years of history of the account that I would be joining. He went through the initial days of struggle, failures, customer interactions, customer culture, stepping stones of success, grooming of people and several aspects of the journey that I absorbed diligently, scribbling down some quick notes in between. He concluded the meeting by saying, 'It is important that you appreciate the background into which you are stepping in, be grateful for all the work put in so far and contribute to this rich culture as you move forward with it.' When someone in a senior role displays this attitude, it automatically drives the others to follow suit and ensure that good practices are kept intact.

EXPERIENCES WORTH REMEMBERING

Cathy is the director of engineering in a company which manufactures electronic equipments. Their unit is one of the oldest in the company with a history dating back to the set up of the company itself. One of the rituals which Cathy drives every alternate week with her team is something which they call 'EWR: experiences worth remembering'. 'This is open to every individual in the team. We welcome them to share "positive experiences worth remembering" which they have been directly part of or those that they might have heard. This could come anywhere from the company. This is followed by appreciating the individuals behind the experience and registering this as a short story. This has been a good way to remember how far and how well we have come along,' she would say.

#In your team and your company, what experiences are getting passed around and remembered?

#GameofDrones

- I have a packed working schedule, and I do not find time to discuss softer aspects of work culture and other things with the seniors of the team.
- I am not very interested in joining team or programme-level meetings; I don't find them relevant to my direct line of work.
    - Even when I attend these meetings, I participate in mute; no one would notice anyway.
- The knowledge-sharing sessions I provide to the new joiners are limited to the project work.
- We have multiple teams within the programme which I am part of but we don't share experiences across. We usually operate in silos and focus on our deliverables.
- The focus in my team is to meet the next milestone and better the previous results, but we don't spend time being thankful and happy about what we have achieved.
- I tend to hear more negative stories than positive ones.

Now discover and evaluate each roadblock. Think of it as a real drone and see how it is doing. Be honest and review how well you are flying it.

☐ **Fully autonomous flight**

☐ **Guided flights**

☐ **Irregular flight path**

☐ **Unwilling to take off**

#KeyResonatingActions

- Organize joint reflection sessions where the entire team or smaller units can come together to practise the art and collectively appreciate the experiences.
- Create success stories contextual to the team and talk about it, especially with new joiners.
- Be very specific on the key strengths of the team (or company) and help everyone connect with those strengths.
- Help the team appreciate the foundation laid out in the past several years and on what milestones the current state of operations are built.
- Create a team identity (digital or otherwise) where key milestones and stories can be documented.
- Talk about key customer meetings and what aspects are being appreciated by customers (and those that are not).
- Constantly discuss the company values, customer values and examples from different teams around these.
- Discuss the weak areas/bottlenecks and encourage the team to contribute to the solutions—discussing issues openly would control the negative gossip and help the team to develop the right behaviours.

#StickyNoteWorthy

When you are grateful, fear disappears and abundance appears.

Tony Robbins

A team which is grateful for the journey made would have the energy to lay sights on the next available peak. Retaining and re-inforcing the winning attributes and behaviours by remembering them often would provide the team the source of inspiration to solve today's problems and continuously evolve to a better stature.

20

THE DEMANDING HILL

Empathetic Leadership

The prince of Stilland was famous for his bad temper and insatiable expectations on others. He got infuriated for trifling matters and showed no empathy to his people. The soldiers and staff of the palace lived in mortal fear of the consequences of his rage and avoided getting into conflict with him. It was best for them to say 'Yes' and get things done without a question.

Apart from this, he was known to be a skilled warrior and, when in the right mood, a compassionate person. But everyone feared him, for they didn't know when he would turn sour and unleash himself upon them. He also detested all the aspects of administration and political affairs.

'You must pay attention, Egar! Your rage and demanding nature are quite popular within the royal chambers and now gaining fame across the kingdom; you must control it. Do you know what they call you behind your back? "The arrogant BISS,"' the king sighed. 'What! Whoever said that will be beheaded. What is BISS?' snapped Egar. 'Then you will end up having a kingdom of dead people and a handful of "Yes men!" around you soon. BISS is your common response for those who would dare to raise a question—Because I said so!' the king replied.

Egar also did not show much interest in meeting with the subjects and understanding the problems of the kingdom. 'Let us appoint wise men who would take care of them, father; our prime minister is an intelligent man; he will solve the problems; why should I be bothered with these?' he remarked.

'If you do not understand your people and empathize with their problems, what kind of king you will be?' the King thumped his fist on the table. 'But these are stupid distractions to me. I would like to be free. I would like to be the best warrior there ever was, and for that I need to train harder and do nothing else,' Egar would argue. 'Then you would have earned your place as a soldier in the army, a great one no doubt, but no more than that,' the king replied. The prince didn't care much as he knew that his father will never let him be a solider; he was to be the future king of Stilland.

One day the king called Egar to his chambers. 'I would like to send you to a friend of mine. He is a wizard by name Slairt and is a powerful one. If you manage to impress him with your dedication to the task he would assign to you, he may teach you the secrets of his magic! This will make you an immensely powerful warrior as you so desire to be,' said the king. Egar was excited. This was the opportunity he longed for—to get away from the monotony of the palace and learn something which will make him unbeatable. He set out to meet this wizard the very next day. 'Remember, he is known to be even more outrageous than you; do not make the mistake of not meeting his expectations, he may curse you,' warned his father. 'There is no task that I cannot accomplish, if I am not distracted,' Egar replied and took off on his horse.

After a long journey which lasted a month, through a difficult terrain, Egar reached the base of the hill on the top of which lived the wizard in a strange-looking house. There was another hill right next to his house which appeared to be alive from a distance. It looked scary and monstrous in the moonlit night. Egar's horse feared something as if it sensed danger. It refused to move forward from that point onwards, and Egar moved to the wizard's house on foot. As Egar approached the house, he saw that the house was leaning on the base of the hill as if it were almost part of it. And the hill seemed to change colour as he approached it, turning bright red. 'I must be tired,' he thought.

Slairt's house was filled with strange-looking items which Egar never saw before. Huge stacks of old manuscripts adorned the walls on one side and the other side had piles of herbs and exotic plants stacked in rows of old wooden cupboards. Egar could hear whispering voices in the house as he entered.

'You have courage making it this far and entering my house,' Slairt sounded cold. He appeared to be leaning onto something which he was working on and spoke without looking at Egar. 'You want to gain power from me, but that comes with great effort, are you willing to risk it?' he demanded the prince. 'I have come all the way to attain something which will make me mighty. I am willing to take up any task as long as I can work on it without distractions,' he humbly replied. 'We shall see to that,' Slairt continued to work. Climb up that winding staircase, you will find your room. Be ready early tomorrow morning, and you shall receive your task.'

'Do you see the waterfall down the hill on the other side?' asked Slairt the next morning. 'Yes, I see now; I did not notice it yesterday, although I could hear the splash of water last night,' Egar replied. 'This Redhill is magical and thirsts for the water from that fall. When someone fetches enough water from the waterfall and pours it on the hill, it melts down and grants a wish. You have to make a pot out of the clay surrounding the waterfall, fetch the water and pour it on the hill, until the hill shrinks and disappears. If you do not pour quickly enough, the hill will grow back!' Slairt explained the task to the horrified prince. 'But this is impossible, I am not a potter and certainly not a lowly slave; what kind of mean task this is!' he was beginning to get angry when he saw Slairt's eyes turn red and he remembered his father's caution. 'My apologies, I have never done this before,' he replied with a calmer tone. 'To achieve what you desire, this is the task, go with it or I will curse you to be my slave for life!' threatened Slairt.

Egar had no choice. He regretted coming out from the safety of his palace. But he was also determined to try. If he could succeed with this task, who knows what unimaginable power he could gain! He saw the bright Redhill which shone brilliantly in the sun light. He hopped down the hill and quickly paced towards the waterfall. As Slairt stated, there was a lot of sticky mud close by and he tried to recollect from his tutors the art of making pots. With each failed attempt he cursed his kingdom, his parents and Slairt for having put him through this ordeal. Nevertheless, he persisted and could make what looked like a crooked container. He smashed into the ground with anger and headed back to Slairt's house as it was nearly dark.

'How many pots of water did you carry today?' demanded Slairt. Egar remembered how a group of servants rushed to take care of him whenever he entered the palace and deep down felt resentful of his behaviour with them. 'I did not carry any; I had too many distractions; the noise of the waterfall is unbearable…,' he complained. 'You will finish the task, or you will not leave this place. Eat the bread which I have reserved for you and get on with the task tomorrow,' replied Slairt.

Egar kept trying each day, but only returned more frustrated. This seemed to be an impossible errand, and he cursed himself for signing up for something so foolish and time-consuming. He imagined that the hill grew bigger than what it was when he saw it for the first time. 'This horrible place is affecting my mind,' he thought. 'At least tell me why you are putting me to such an impossible expectation; I was expecting the task to be aligned to my fighting skills; this doesn't make sense to me!' he pleaded. 'You will do it "Because I said so,"' snapped Slairt. Egar remembered his father's words and felt ashamed of his behaviour with his people.

After what seemed like ages, he succeeded to make a pot decent enough to hold water, but the pot needed to dry to carry any water at all. The place near the waterfall was too humid, so he decided to make multiple pots which he could dry in the sun. Once the pots were ready, he finally set out to take a potful of water to the hill. As he poured the water on the walls of the hill, it boomed 'more!!!' like a voice that came from the middle of the hill. And the water vanished as if he poured it on raging fire.

'What a monstrous hill!' he thought fuming with anger. 'More!!!' the hill boomed again. Egar repeated the drill several times in the day, but the hill responded with a demand for more water. He could see no signs of the hill melting down. He decided to question the wizard that night. 'Slairt! Please tell me if this is an arrangement by my father to keep me hostage to this place? I am working on an errand which no man can accomplish. I am not afraid of your curse, but I want to know the truth,' he asked. 'Your father is a noble king, do not dare doubt his intent,' Slairt replied. Egar grew more restless hearing this.

As he continued his painful walk up and down the hill carrying pots of water to the demanding hill, Egar also reflected on the problems of his people which he paid half attention to. He decided to get more involved in resolving their issues when he, if ever, got back. 'More!!!' demanded the hill as it showed no signs of shrinking down. 'I will conquer you!' Egar yelled back with determination and not as much with anger this time. He saw that a small tip of the hill chip away as a strong gust of wind blew fiercely. 'I will conquer you,' he replied calmly and marched to the waterfall with his pots.

As he poured pot after pot of water day after day, he started to gain more composure in the errand. He started early, paced himself through the day and tried to move more water every day than he did the day before. He spent the nights trying to reconcile with himself and the life he spent so far. 'How demanding have I been with everyone around!' he thought. After few more days, he completely lost himself in the errand so much so that he lost sense of the surroundings and the external distractions. His only purpose was to keep moving and conquering the demanding hill. Whenever he heard 'more!!!' from the hill, it reminded him of his demanding self and how he behaved with all around him. He so wanted to kill the voice completely.

After what appeared to be more than several months of persistent effort, Egar felt that the voice softened; it did not sound demanding like before, although it still said 'more' with each pot of water being emptied. Egar also felt that he was assisting the hill to melt down and free it from its misery of the demand. It felt strange but peaceful to think this way. He felt more energized and that day he poured more water than he ever did before and by the end of the day, he could see that the Redhill was starting to shrink. Overjoyed with what he saw, Egar emptied some more pots of water all through the night and by the next day lay at the foot of the flattened hill completely exhausted but contented.

Slairt rushed out of the house to assist the prince. 'You have accomplished the task, Egar; you have overcome the Redhill!' he exclaimed in joy. 'And I feel fulfilled too; I do not need any powers; I would like to get back to my father and my people and correct the wrongs I have done,' Egar humbly replied. 'But you have gained immense power, Egar. The Redhill was but a reflection of the demanding hill within you. The waterfall represented precious stream of life—of yourself and your people—which you were demanding so much of without melting down. This errand was a means to conquer the Redhill in yourself and appreciate all that is around you. The Redhill was magical indeed—you are now truly unconquerable since you have conquered yourself and your distractions in the bargain and discovered your true strength,' replied Slairt. Egar bowed in response and prepared to leave for his kingdom.

#WorkplaceWhispers

The ever-mounting expectations of the market, constraints under which one needs to operate and need to drive continuous motivation within the teams to get the job done (without falling prey to the first two forces) make the modern-day leadership not everyone's dream endeavour. Leaders are constantly pushed to make difficult choices and run a profitable business, keep competition at bay and at the same time make further investments to prepare for the future. In all this bargain, one choice that leaders cannot afford to lose out on is to keep their team close and make them feel part of the journey.

THE TRANSPARENT LEADER

A senior leader from one of the APAC customers who I worked with said this during an interaction: 'Once in a while there are ad hoc requirements, and everybody understands that. But apart from such unplanned asks, my team usually knows what I expect from them and when—both in terms of quality and scope.'

Consider the following common whispers at the workplace:

1. 'This will not fly; I know what my boss expects. We need to put in more effort and improve the quality of this deliverable before we could take it to her.'

Vs

2. 'How could he say that he is disappointed with my work? Should I read his mind as to what he wanted. I tried to do something despite such unclear expectations and still he says that he is disappointed. Well I am disappointed too!'

I hope the second whisper above is not so common at your place. It is a joy for the team to work with a firm belief that they understand the expectations of their leader. When this is not the case and there is a mismatch between expectation vs actual output, instead of snapping at the team with 'I *expected* you to do better,' this can be used as an opportunity by the leader to connect with the team and work with them further. Let us look at two approaches on how leaders can get the team to participate willingly even when the expectations are high.

THE TEAM ALWAYS ANSWERS THE CALL

There was a high stakes large programme which was headed towards a disaster. The milestones promised to customer were being missed constantly; the quality was poor; and the teams were under severe stress. Management decided to bring in a senior leader to take control of the programme and turn it around. One of the statements he made in the first leadership meeting was on these lines, 'Together, we should make a choice today—to turn this around—for ourselves more than anything else. There is no other way. And for that we should align better, push each other more, but also take care of each other and expect nothing but highest levels of quality from each other. I will also have grand expectations on you, and I expect you to return the favour—place your highest expectations on me, and I will try to meet them as much as I can....' The programme was turned around in a year's time, and it was one of the toughest experiences ever for the team, but also most gratifying. They knew that they had a leader who would stand by them and that enabled them to give it their all.

Once a connect is made, and the leader is willing to stand up to the expectations of the team, they will play along and answer the call of the leader, no matter how tough the expectation is.

EASIER DONE THAN SAID...

Mr Jonathan took over as the director of a large programme responsible for delivering analytics services to a major retail customer. He was told when he took over the programme that the unit was performing poorly with a lot of customer complaints. In the initial few days Jonathan understood that the teams on the ground were bored and disinterested. On further observation, he found that that was a reflection of how the leadership team was behaving. He called them all to a meeting room and showed them a white board with a table and names of his team including his name, with the title 'The Calling'.

'Let's play a game. We agree to a start time at work. And we will watch out for each other. If you come in to work at the agreed time and find that I didn't make it in yet, you will call me from my work phone to my mobile and put a count in this table at the intersection of your name and mine. If I come in earlier than you, I would do the same. We will see in a month's time who is getting called the most. I know I will have to contend with all of you,' he winked.

For the next one month, Jonathan would come in a few minutes ahead of the start time and go for a quick round in the work zones. He would come in late on purpose once in a while to lose out to his team and get them to score over him. In a couple of months, the table stood bare, with no counts in it, and the expectation was met even without asking for it explicitly.

Playing along with the team and living the behaviours which need to be nurtured first hand are effective ways to drive change in the team.

#GameofDrones

AS AN INDIVIDUAL

- I do not like conflict and want to be on the good books of my manager all the time.
- I tend to say 'Yes' to whatever my manager says; he must surely know better.
- I don't understand some of the expectations but accept the task given anyway.
- I tend to gossip about the bad decisions of my manager with other colleagues, since I cannot give direct feedback.
- When I get critical feedback from my manager, for no fault of mine, I tend to go into a shell and disconnect with the rest of the team.

AS A LEADER

- I have high expectations on my team because I know it is in their best interests. I don't put the effort to clarify this to them though, as my intent is noble.
- I have the highest expectations on my team all the time, but I don't always check if they are equipped to deliver; they should let me know if they want help.
- I get a hard time from the senior management, so there is no harm in passing it on to my team.
- I cannot tolerate anyone from the team challenging my decisions.
- I see three sections in my team—those who always like what I say, those who always don't like what I say and those who don't really care but follow anyway.

Now discover and evaluate each roadblock. Think of it as a real drone and see how it is doing. Be honest and review how well you are flying it.

- [ ] **Fully autonomous flight**
- [ ] **Guided flights**
- [ ] **Irregular flight path**
- [ ] **Unwilling to take off**

#KeyResonatingActions

AS AN INDIVIDUAL

- Build a personal brand by being consistent in speaking up, asking questions and seeking/sharing feedback.
- Discuss challenges upfront and solicit needed support to meet the delivery objectives.
- When critical feedback is given, seek to understand better—show interest in receiving feedback and request your manager (or whoever is giving feedback) to work with you in bringing about the necessary improvements. This will be seen as a sign of respect and willingness on your side to participate.
- Try to be honest in every conversation rather than trying to please your manager. Managers will rely on honest voices in the long run, even if they tend to get annoyed in the short one.

AS A LEADER

- Use every opportunity/forum to let them discover who you are as a leader—your thoughts about them, your big picture view and why you do what you do. Understanding the leader is an essential aspect of responding to expectations.

- Have a keen sense of interest in your team—how they do what they do, how much effort goes behind a deliverable, what the cost of an expectation is and whether they are enabled enough to perform.
- Be especially balanced when the team already knows that they have messed up and they have every reason to expect tough behaviour from you.
- Position the team ahead of yourself before senior management or other forums of visibility during the times of success.
- Have explicit 'listening sessions' where feedback from the team can be heard in an unbiased manner.
- Be open to discuss the constraints and what is possible/not possible.

#StickyNoteWorthy

One cannot hire a hand; the whole man comes with it.

Peter Drucker

It is easy to be composed and compassionate when things are going well and the team is riding a wave of success. But it is also when things get tough and there is pressure from all directions that the team looks to the leader (their immediate manager) for support, compassion and direction. This provides a good opportunity to bring your team on your side, which is both practical and essential to get out of a tough situation.

Time and energy (effort) of associates are precious gifts which a leader gets endowed with, and those should not be squandered under the guise of 'unclear and high expectations' or haughty behaviour by the leader under any circumstances.

21

THE HIDDEN TREASURE

'And there are some treasures which remain an enigma; we know nothing of them; they lay out there, undiscovered … and take along with them some of the finest archaeologists,' concluded Professor Harrison about the attempts to uncover the lost treasure of Dulu as they called it. There was a momentary pause in the classroom and then the usual buzz as the students eagerly waited for the next break.

Two students remained seated in their place and spoke softly to each other without moving.

'Josh, you are from that place, aren't you? Do you believe the story? Do you recollect any stories of the treasure?' enquired Robin. 'Shh! So much for letting you in on my background, I don't want to talk about it and I know nothing of any treasure; I am surprised that this is recorded formally in academics!' said Josh.

'Professor, I would like to know more about Dulu, beyond what's written in that paper,' Robin called out to Professor Harrison as he proceeded to leave the room. 'Well, I am glad you do, but I have nothing more to offer, I am afraid. Just that the last known person as per the records that went to Dulu and never returned was Wilson Roy, almost a hundred years ago. All we know from the last of his records which were recovered from a local library at the time pointed to a priceless treasure in the grasslands and forests. Several attempts were made until recently, with most advanced equipment, to crack into the Dulu region. There are mentions of pieces of diamonds, some rocks with rich minerals and some tribal pieces of art being recovered, but nobody could get to the source. It is a dense temperate forest region, and the best teams of archaeologists and geologists couldn't get past the fringes of Dulu. It is an interesting field assignment though, if you both care to pick it up.'

Josh did a motion with both his hands instinctively. 'Why did you do that?' asked Professor Harrison. 'Oh, it is a sign of respect in the place he comes from,' blurted Robin and bit his tongue realizing his mistake. 'Interesting … and what place would that be?' enquired Harrison. 'It's nothing, professor, I was just stretching my hands; Robin gets funny sometimes without reason,' said Josh. Professor Harrison frowned at both and left the room.

Ever since Josh joined the Queensland college, he developed a reputation of being 'that weird guy'. His mannerisms and accent stood him out. Robin was the only one who embraced him and very soon they became good friends. Although Josh was disinterested in going back to Dulu, with unrelenting persistence from Robin, they both took up the field assignment and landed in a village bordering the Dulu forest region.

'I can't believe I got fooled into joining you on this madness,' said Josh as they drank the hot tea served by the inn keeper of the village. The wannabe archaeologists wandered the area and tried to interact with the locals to find some clues to the treasure with no luck. They sighted a mysterious old man who seemed to come out once in a while from the forest and interact with the villagers. He would bring them fresh fruits and forest herbs, and quickly disappear back into the forest. The boys had their chance when the old man dropped by their inn to give medicines to the inn keeper and quickly followed him as he rushed into the forest.

They were surprised with his agility despite his age as they saw him disappear in a short time. Very soon they both found themselves quite away from the village and lost in the forest. However, Josh seemed oddly comfortable, as if his native instincts had turned themselves on in this habitat. 'Feels like I know the place, although I swear to you, I have never been here before,' he said and slowly lead the way. The forest floor was harsh with dense shrubs and overgrown ferns, thorny cactus-like plants, red oaks and pines, and strange looking rocks. Robin had this weird feeling that some of the plants stood out like they were making a sign with their branches. 'A few kilometres north from here, we should hit water,' professed Josh. 'What! Where did that come from? Did you develop some extra sensory abilities around here? Don't spook me out, Josh,' cried Robin. 'I don't know!' he did a hand movement. After a few more hours, Robin started to get extremely weak and delirious. 'I am seeing fairies I think,' he giggled. 'Keep moving, Rob, we are very close.'

They trudged along and soon enough hit what appeared to be a small freshwater lake with the sound of a whooshing waterfall nearby. 'Are those fairies too? Or monsters?' Robin kept gazing aimlessly and talking nonstop. 'Quiet!' said Josh and did a sign with his hands and bowed to the approaching young man. 'I swear I saw this guy somewhere,' said Robin again.

'You two stubborn kids! How did you make it this far? The forest could have killed you by night, ahha the Duluai … here tell your friend to chew this quickly…,' he gave some red leaves for Robin to eat. 'What is a Duluai?' Robin almost yelled as the leaves brought him back to normalcy. 'It means a boy of Dulu, and be quiet, you will disturb the forest; take to that corner and rest; we will speak tomorrow,' he said and left.

'Several attempts were made to discover the treasure of Dulu over the past centuries,' said the young man the next morning. 'Many smart archaeologists and scientists with advanced equipment, even with drone surveillance and lasers shooting at the forest bed', he paused and smiled.

'But there is a treasure, right? There are some sightings of rare metals, and some diamonds even,' interrupted Robin. Josh did a hand movement which appeared as if he gestured Robin to shut up. 'You are a true descendant, Duluai, it is coming to you slowly,' Josh heard the young man saying. 'What did he tell you? What language was that?' asked Robin. 'What? You didn't understand what he just said? Didn't he speak English?' asked Josh. 'No, I did not, Duluai, I spoke your native tongue; the outsider will not get it,' again the young man replied in the strange language.

'Please speak in English; we want to uncover the treasure and enlighten the world; we do not want it,' pleaded Robin. 'You cannot uncover the treasure by being who you are; you need to become one with the place and learn the Dulu spirit. Else you will forget everything I tell you once you leave the forest,' smiled the young man. 'What about Josh? He is a native, would he remember?' asked Robin. 'He would if he chooses to remain true to Dulu. There is some part of him which retained that spirit and helped him find his way back here, else the forest would have rejected both of you and led you into a deadly trap.'

'Do you know what happened to Wilson Roy and the other archaeologists who came by, and what is the story of Dulu?' asked Josh.

'I am bound by the land to tell the story when someone from this place asks me. So I will tell you Josh.

> Wilson Roy came here almost a hundred years ago with a large team and a lot of equipment. There were others too, and their purpose was to uncover the treasure of Dulu. They spent a lot of time taking samples and studying the earth. They even tried to lure the natives of Dulu with gifts and comforts and better life. Some of

the natives fell for it and left, but once they decided to leave, they couldn't help the explorers understand Dulu anymore. So the place remained an enigma for a long time. While the others tried and left, Wilson Roy was the stubborn one; he arranged for his living in the bordering village from where you two came and tried making expeditions on his own into the forest. He used to make notes of such expeditions and post it in the nearby libraries; once in a while he would find an odd stone, a diamond and that was enough for more explorers to pour in,' the young man paused.

'And they repeated the process—take samples, lure the natives, treat them like they are some strange animals and use them to get to what they thought was the treasure. It took a couple of years or so for Wilson to realize that he was doing it all wrong…,' he paused again and Robin noticed that he was making some hand signs to Josh and Josh responded likewise. 'What happened! What did Wilson do differently?' asked Robin.

'He realized that the knowledge of the treasure could not be had by drawing the natives out and *making them something they are not, but by learning their language, by treating them with respect.* But it was not easy. The natives were not easy to gain trust of. It took another couple of years of persistence and pleading before he was accepted into the tribe and passed the test of Dulu,' said the young man.

'So that was it, was it so simple? Learn the language, pass the test and find the treasure! Doesn't seem so hard, what's the test?' asked Robin.

'To drink from that lake. Once you are allowed to learn the Dulu and their ways, the natives will allow you to drink from that spring, and if there is any malicious intent, the lake takes away the spirit of Dulu, the person forgets everything and gets thrown out of the forest,' smiled the young man.

'Ah! That's why no one knows what the treasure really is?' enquired Robin. 'Yes, several came, very few realized the source of knowledge and out of those who did and tried, none succeeded. But Wilson succeeded and he chose to become one with the natives, that's why he didn't come back to your world.'

'And we think we are advanced and smart and treat those, for instance, those who don't speak even good English, as idiots!' remarked Robin. 'But you were always different, Rob, you accepted me for who I am. You saw sense in all my weirdness,' Josh put his hand on Robin's shoulder.

'But why did the natives leave? There are so few of you now! Why did my grandparents leave?' asked Josh. 'Lack of belief in their true nature, *someone comes and tells you that you are a "root-fruit-eating stupid tribal" and they believed so.* Some got lured by others, promise of "a better life" outside, many reasons. *Sticking to one's roots seems to get put to test occasionally in the history of time.* Why did you come back, Josh?' asked the young man.

'Due to Rob, he pulled me, but now that I am here, I feel I belong here. Will I forget everything I learnt outside if I decide to stay here or vice versa?' asked Josh. 'That depends, you can remain true to Dulu no matter where you are and be a part of it. And you are a fine example of that fact. *Do not be ashamed of who you are at the core, and always respect others.* But, of course, there are benefits of staying here,' the young man chuckled.

'We are leaving without finding out what the treasure of Dulu is all about; I feel so disappointed after coming this far,' remarked Robin as they were lead to the edge of the forest by the young man the next day. As Josh and Robin walked a few paces out of the forest, they heard the voice of the old man they met at the inn a few days ago, 'Oh, I am sure Josh understands what the treasure is all about by the time we part ways.' They turned around to see the old man in place of the young one who was with them all along. 'The farther I go from the forest, the older I get,' he smiled.

'Wilson Roy! This really is you,' cried Robin. 'Yes, sirs! And Robin you will forget all of this soon. Josh you will too, if you decide to harm Dulu in any way or part ways with the spirit of Dulu,' said Wilson.

'I will bring back my grandparents here, they will be so happy. Thank you for sharing your story, sir—there is a great lesson for us all—*one gets to the real treasure hidden beneath someone by learning to speak their language and truly thinking good of them, and not by intelligence, deceit or even advanced methods.* We miss this simple lesson in our daily affairs and draw comparison, contrast and conceit,' he said.

'And some hidden treasures … ahem … talents of people are never discovered due to lack of proper attempts … *speaking the right language with them*, I am glad I didn't give up on you, Josh,' said Robin.

'True, Rob. It would have saved years of labour and cost if only the smart explorers realized this. Proud to be a Duluai,' said Josh as they both bid farewell to Wilson and watched him disappear into the forest.

#WorkplaceWhispers

Take a moment and reflect on this—are there people in your phone book (let's limit it to the list of colleagues at work only) whose calls you would pick up more often than not, and then there are those who you would prefer not to pick up, given a choice? And for the ones in the former category (I hope your manager is one of them!), what about them do you think makes you give them this liberty?

Isn't it natural for most of us that we tend to open up and contribute more in an environment where we believe that our words will be respected/paid attention to and we are understood for who we are and what we say?

Every individual interacts best when they are in their *comfort zone* (which depends on one's *diversity factor*—cultural background, upbringing, sensitivity, self-image and motivation, among other things). Successful leaders have a knack of understanding this and making a connect via the right language and respect to the individual. And once they make the connect, it becomes easy to draw out the best from the team.

On the other hand, when this connect is not made, and the leader places an expectation, there is a cold response; no one opens up and remains guarded of their ideas and inputs. Most treasures of the team (skills, ideas, points of view) remain subdued and inaccessible this way.

Here are a couple of fictional cases which highlight the aspect of diversity and which one needs to overcome the outward barriers to access the true potential of the team.

ATTIRE-LY POSSIBLE

Subramanya Sarma is one of the senior architects and domain experts in an organization. An introvert and perfectionist by nature, he prefers keeping to himself and is very focused on work. But that's not what gets him the attention or sometimes the lack of it. 'People hesitate coming to me openly or joke around with me like the way they do with others. Once they start interacting with me, things get normal, but the hesitation is always there, and I have now got used to it. Of course, some of it has got to do with my tight manners and body language, but also, my cultural attire—the long-drawn tilak on my forehead and the short tuft on the back of my head. A few told me in a good-natured manner as to why don't I get rid of those, as they clearly call for undue attention in a modern workplace. I tell them that there is a profound meaning behind those symbols in my culture, I feel stronger with them,' he says.

This is not limited to Sarma alone; it could be a Hassan Shoeb or a Jose Pedro. Every individual is a spark of a rich culture and heritage before they became an associate at a workplace. Their cultural orientation and the associated mannerisms must not only be respected but also cherished and applauded.

LINGUAL BARRIERS: A HARD PROBLEM OVERCOME

There was a tense environment as the issue at hand was a severe one and already two days were lost—one of the major business application was down and no one could crack the problem. A cross-functional team was deployed with representation from the SMEs from different companies involved in supporting the application, and they were working on this problem in a war room set-up.

Finally, an expert was identified by the product company and he was supposed to be the best in the continent. There was only one challenge—he was not very good with English and had a slight stammer. The head of the product company introduced the expert and urged everyone to cooperate with him: 'If he cannot solve it, then no one in our company can,' he said. The expert introduced himself and said, 'My English not okay. But it's okay, you follow my instruction. I am proud of what I bring to you, and it's not language for today, let's work.'

Although the team hesitated initially, within less than 30 minutes, they got into a rhythm. For an non-expert, that conversation would have looked like gibberish, but the teams overlooked the disability of the expert and focused on his instructions to the letter. His stammer didn't matter nor his imperfect English. The problem was fixed in the next couple of hours, and the systems were restored.

#GameofDrones

AS AN INDIVIDUAL

- I hesitate most of the times to share my point of view in a forum; I think my frequency doesn't match with the others.
- I am unable to follow the pace of conversation during meetings; they look like they are targeted only to a few individuals in the team—I wonder why all of us are invited.
- I feel out of place in the team; although I am very good at what I do, I am not so good with English and striking conversations.
- Although I don't interact much with them, I have a low opinion on certain individuals in the team; I may not work with them so well in projects, if we are put together.

AS A LEADER

- I am not aware of the distinct backgrounds of my team.
- I tend to get along with some of my team members who are from the same cultural background or same frequency of thinking as I and not so much with others.
- I don't see good participation from the team when I solicit ideas; the same few individuals speak often.
- I do not put much effort on why my team behaves the way they do; I tend to think that their capability is low.

- I use sophisticated language; whenever I find a new phrase or a cool management jargon, I throw it at my team.

Now discover and evaluate each roadblock. Think of it as a real drone and see how it is doing. Be honest and review how well you are flying it.

- ☐ **Fully autonomous flight**
- ☐ **Guided flights**
- ☐ **Irregular flight path**
- ☐ **Unwilling to take off**

#KeyResonatingActions

AS AN INDIVIDUAL

- Be proud of your diversity and background; it brings strength to the team—if you don't back yourself up, no one else would spend the time to do that.
- Talk about it in team connects and other forums so that the rest of the team can appreciate it too.
- Focus on skills needed to get the job done, and convey your points of view at your own pace.
- Be open to feedback, and ask questions if something is not understood.
- Be interested in learning about each other's strengths and weaknesses in the team.

AS A LEADER

- Use simple language and different styles with different team members if you can manage.

- Help the team participate, be their greatest translator and bridge in the team to connect them even with each other.
- Continuously expand your circle of the team which you can connect with.
- Be persistent with and enthusiastic about your team; trust cannot be solicited in a rush.
- Organize meet-ups where team members with diverse backgrounds can be brought together and share about themselves in a semi-formal/informal forum.
- Constantly be mindful of and work towards breaking the superiority/inferiority biases in the team.

#StickyNoteWorthy

Diversity & Inclusion needs to be something that every single employee at the company has a stake in.

Bo Young Lee

Embracing diversity and tracking the diversity factor are increasingly becoming common in organizations. And the reason for that is not just to look good on books but with the realization that diversity sparks and propels innovation.

Globalization and glocalization are also driving adaptive behaviours within companies which are aiming to scale and grow. The ability to expand into a market which is different from the home country (or even region) would mean excelling at the ability to interact with and impress consumers, partners and suppliers with diverse backgrounds. And this applies at a micro level too, in the day to day conversations and interactions at work. Instead of pushing each other to comply to commonality (with due regard to standards and regulations which have to be complied to), if only the focus can be shifted to inspiring each other in glorious diversity, abundant treasures can be unlocked.

22

AT THE CORE OF IT ALL

In ancient times, somewhere in the forests of Central Europe lived a tribe by name Beertas. They created a colony in the deep forests of the land and preferred to stay away from the rest of the civilization. The kingdoms around these forests heard of folklore which spoke about special abilities of the Beertas and how they had figured out a way of life intertwined with nature.

Of the many great skills the Beertas were known to possess, they were also known to be experts at identifying medicinal herbs and gathering honey from the most exquisite beeswax. One of the lesser known reasons why the tribes were let on their own without being conquered by the neighbouring kingdoms was the reliance on the Beertas to cure certain deadly diseases by sharing rare herbs and rare honey extracted from impossible locations of the land. 'They speak to the bees and are led by them to these locations,' said the village people that lived closer to the forests.

The Beertas relied on each other and led a life by 'the code of the tribe' with a sacred mission to pass down their *ancestral knowledge to the next generations*. Children were carefully observed to sense the budding talent and further coached by expert teachers of the tribe towards one of the rare skills which helped Beertas survive and thrive. Young boys and girls grew up into 'friends of birds', 'friends of animals', 'friends of plants' or 'friends of bees' also known as bee talkers. Only once in a long time they had one child who was born with a gift to conquer all the four skills. Such men/women grew up to head the tribe and took responsibility of the Beerta tribe as long as they lived. Kookah was the reining leader of the tribe at the time and grew into an expert in all the four disciplines of the tribe.

Kookah followed his predecessors in organizing his administration into different camps each headed by a leader. The camps themselves were organized by the specific skills which they nurtured and had experts in charge of teaching and further research. Kookah had his best man in Religo, who was one of the most respected elders and was considered the wisest man of the Beerta tribe.

It must have been the irony of contrast, *diversity brought with it a sense of natural competition,* and there were debates between the young ones as to which camp was the strongest. 'We talk to the forest and help in building shelter and finding medicines; ours is the most sacred and sensitive craft,' said the friends of the plant. 'We protect the land; we speak to the birds and bring food but also get early warning of the dangers from beyond. We are the guardians,' said the friends of the birds. 'Look who is talking, who speaks to the wild animals and secures the perimeter, who brings the sacred flesh for building strength in our young, we are the fearless,' said the ones that were friends with animals. 'One of you should come with our next expedition of bee hunting, you wouldn't last half a day. We scale the mountains or the tallest of trees to secure the most exquisite honey and keep you all healthy; our warriors are strongest, fastest and swift like the bee. We never tire!' said the bee talkers.

'As long as they don't take to arms against each other, Religo,' laughed Kookah as he gathered his camp heads by the council fire. It was customary for the camp heads to meet every full moon day to talk about the proceedings and any matters which needed attention.

'The code binds them stronger than their ego, Kookah!' smiled Religo. 'However, in all this contrast and competition as to who is better, they are missing the joy of subtleties in their skills and the vast store of ancestral knowledge which they can gain.'

'Something seems to be bothering you, Nola,' frowned Kookah. Nola was the head of the bee talkers, and it was said that she was more a bee herself than a human.

'Same as the other camps, we thrive on learning every single trick and custom of our ancients, mastering it, doing further improvements and passing it to our young. But the young in our camp are growing more impatient, grabbing a few good tricks, and filling their stores to glory, no space for more wax in their combs…,' she mumbled into bee language.

The other camp heads smiled sympathetically and nodded in admission. One could count the lines on the forehead of Religo as the moonlight swept past the forestland for a brief moment before a rogue cloud pulled the blinds. 'You are a wise teacher, Nola, you certainly know how to empty the combs as a wise ancient hunter of the honey,' smiled Religo enquiringly. 'Inspire them to learn more, learn everything, eh?'

'Speaking to the bees is a special and sensitive skill. Speed, strength and patience, all at once. Not every bee speaks easy, the young ones learn to speak with one or two varieties, and they fetch the same honey,' she shot her words like bee stings.

Kookah remembered his time with Nola when he was being taught. She used to say, 'There are countless types of bees, Kookah, you need to develop the sense to speak to every one of them to truly master the art. You should never fill your comb easy, *always keep room for more learning; the more you clear your room, the more you will be fed with new knowledge,*' he was brought back from his thoughts with the cry of a baby in a distant camp.

'Kookah was tough to teach too as a kid,' recollected Nola, 'Although he was the special one, it did not come through easy. It took extraordinary efforts to get to him and train him across all the skills,' she smiled. 'But not everyone is Kookah, and I don't have the same strength as I used to, although you may not notice my age,' she winked at Religo who was also as old as her. 'Yes, the special honey which you don't share with anyone else, that hides your true age,' teased a camp head.

Nola ignored the comment and continued, 'I rely on the trainers which I have trained earlier and they complain that the young ones don't give them a chance to empty their knowledge,' she sighed.

'Before I say anything further, I would like to ask the other camp heads too, how are you handling this in your camps?' Religo asked.

'The learning is good, but not appreciated by the young ones, only 1 in 10 are truly catching the spirit of the flighted ones,' said Akiro the camp head for the friends of birds. 'Some of them think that it is useless to connect; they would like to exert their might and kill the animals,' said the other camp head they called Tora.

As if to set the stage for the wise one to speak, the huge cloud drifted away to allow the white light of the moon shine brightly on Religo, as Kookah looked at him intently. 'This is not the first time we face this clog in the history of our tribe. Every once in a while we hit a point where we find it hard to pass on the baton of our rich knowledge and the answer to this problem, for generations, has always been the same…,' he looked intently at the crackling fire and announced, '…fire!!!'

Nola smiled as she leaned back in place on her stone pedestal covered with soft grass and feathers twined with large leaves. The other camp heads still looked confused.

'*It takes a spark, good wood and nice breeze to light up a fire…*,' said Kookah as he looked at Religo. 'Even with my gifts I had problems with learning. All the problems that our young ones are going through today and several more.' Kookah looked far into the dark forest recollecting his memories from childhood. 'I had sparks of brilliance, there were moments when I picked up a skill quickly and then I would look for applause and appreciation. If I did not get enough of it, I would go numb and not show interest again. The motivation would die down. I would just be happy with what I had and behave arrogantly with everyone around me,' he said.

'Unimaginable! How did they teach you the four skills then and how did you master them so well?' asked Akiro.

'Religo and Nola believed that I had the right material—the raw ability. But to truly generate the fire of learning in me, they needed a spark—right challenges—and some gentle breeze. They found several sparks along the way, sometimes they were generating them, and sometimes we got lucky,' he continued. Religo coughed softly looking at the confused faces of Akiro and Tora.

'First one was by chance—we received word from the neighbouring kingdom that there was an outbreak of a certain yellow fever which had put every able-bodied citizen on the bed and the kingdom had stalled. Nola knew of a rare species of honey which could help fight fevers like that one, but that was incredibly difficult to hunt down. This was an ideal opportunity to test the mettle of Kookah and she took a chance. But one thing that Kookah didn't mention explicitly in the fire metaphor—*all the three should meet together to generate fire, the spark, the breeze and the material that can burn,'* Religo took a pause and looked at Nola.

'I asked Kookah if he had the courage to join me in a death-defying hunt to get the red-mud honey from the hives in the caves behind the waterfall on the edge of the Sneka mountains. This would be his chance to show off yet another time, but it would mean letting go of everything else and take to hard practice,' she said.

'At first, it was the pull of glory, I wanted to show off to other kids. But I quickly understood that it required me to use all the knowledge I had gained and learn so much more. But once we were on the quest, it was Nola's appreciation that kept me going. "Swifter than a deer you run, excellent leaps Kookah … there you picked up the right scent, incredible focus … haven't seen anyone else climb the tree so fast…." *It was much more than just saying something as disconnected as "good job!"* She "exactly knew what and how to appreciate with every move I made." She was the gentle breeze which I needed to sustain the flame,' added Kookah.

'Before I knew I was lost in the quest. It took us four full moons to get to the comb and I have seen the magic of bee hunting and the extent of skill that Nola possessed during this time. I wanted to learn it all and she was more than willing to give it away. If reaching the hive was one challenge, getting the honey was a completely different one,' smiled Kookah.

'"One sting would kill you instantly," Nola said as we approached the hive. "We need to observe their cycle, wait to see if their comb is full and if you read them right, they will allow you to partake some of their wax. Focus on the activity, Kookah, these bees have a deadly sting, but they are the most responsible too. They won't hurt you as long as you don't show ill intentions towards them." The next few days I learnt some of my most precious lessons on the bee talk from Nola, and I had this feeling that the bees were listening too as she spoke about them with such respect and affection. And one day it was our turn to get what we came for. "Do not cut, the bees have shown you where to draw the comb out, see that fissure? Gently pull from the side. I will watch you do it. No one has attempted this in a 100 years, Kookah." I knew that she wouldn't let me die of a bee sting after all this training and did exactly as told, but as I turned back with the piece of the comb 50 bees stung at my back at once, sending a shot of pain as if I was getting struck by lightning. I could still see the smile on the face of Nola before I fell unconscious,' Kookah took a deep breath of the fresh breeze of the night.

'It was the mark of the red mud; they had accepted Kookah as one of their own and initiated him to receive the rest of the knowledge,' said Nola proudly.

'So Religo, is it sufficient to throw challenges to get the young ones interested?' asked Tora. 'Sometimes be the spark, and sometimes be the breeze, but always stay close, show them exquisitely the joy of our ancient learning, appreciate them closely, and yes when the wood in them is ready to burn, ignite the spark,' said Religo.

'It takes great effort to achieve such feats, and our tribe has very few teachers left who are capable of doing that,' said Nola.

'What did you train me for?' smiled Kookah. 'My gifts are not for me to take them to my grave and you taught me that the destiny of the special skills is to impact extraordinary learning. It is my duty to get our young ones feel the warmth of our ancestral knowledge inside of them. Bring forth the ones who you think are your best in each of your camps and we will work together to craft their game,' said Kookah.

'It will tire you out, Kookah; these young ones are certainly not as stubborn as you were, but they are not to be taken lightly,' said Nola. 'Yet you did not give up on me, and some of the other elders of the tribe. Religo, is it time to summon the Beerdareh and initiate the ceremony?' asked Kookah. Beerdareh is called by the Beerta head to launch a series of impossible challenges to aggregate and preserve the most precious items from the forest as a showcase to the young ones of the tribe.

'I will take the best of each from your camps, including some of your trainers, on the quest and show them the amazing hidden wonders and the power of our ancient knowledge. Let me warn you, *if they do not have the right wood in them, the quest will burn them down;* pick the right ones and prepare them, *preparation is key to appreciate and receive our ancient knowledge...,'* said Kookah as he left the place in excitement.

'All that effort that you put to train him paid off eh, Nola?' smirked Religo. 'Yes! Let the fire in Kookah continue to burn and light several more, leading from the front,' she replied.

#WorkplaceWhispers

It is widely accepted that driving continuous learning and innovation is one of the top challenges faced by organizations. Even while selecting partners or investing in long-term relationships, one of the essential attributes under consideration is the ability of the partner organization to have a robust learning/skill generating and innovation framework in place. No one would risk associating with a partner or vendor who is not continuously learning and innovating.

There are broadly two categories of learning which organizations have to tackle:

- Learning needed to sustain the operations of the company and capture incremental growth.
    - o Constant on-job learning—seniors training juniors, developing skills to tackle market/customer demands (hiring would only cater to a minor percentage of needed demand)
    - o Gaining deep contextual knowledge of the environment and line of business
    - o Knowledge transition which comes along with the movement of associates
    - o Regulatory, compliance-learning requirements

Most organizations have deep structures and processes to ensure that this becomes part of the operations itself. However, not all organizations/teams manage to sustain the high levels of quality for a long time. As good people leave and the context (both hard skills and soft skills) gained is scattered, teams tend to go through a downward spiral and get overtaken by a competitor.

- Learning needed to push the boundaries forward:
    - o Constant experimentation and innovation
    - o Unlearning and relearning (process redefinition, better way of doing things)

This is both based/built on the first category of learning, as well as actively experimenting in newer areas (depending on the line of work, culture, ethics and investment muscle of the organization).

And for both the above categories of learning to succeed, beyond the processes and frameworks set up in an organization, it would require deeply motivated individuals and leaders who make it their noble mission to learn and train.

A MEANS TO CONNECT

Associates are constantly looking for fulfilment beyond monetary gains. They seek someone (an expert mentor) to work with them and help them build themselves. Given the plethora of learning paths, active mentoring is seen as a value add by the associates and for leadership, this is a great way to connect with the teams. 'When I get an appreciation from my manager who I consider as an expert in this field of work, I feel a sense of accomplishment. He also brings in SMEs constantly to review our work, and it feels great when they look at what we do and appreciate our thoroughness,' says Srikanth (name changed), a network field engineer.

THE DEMANDS OF APPRECIATION

'It is particularly important that associates in leadership roles constantly spend time in learning the key elements of the lines of work which they oversee, even if it is not possible to gain expertise at everything. Without this, they will not be able to keenly appreciate the work being done by their team. It will always be a "good job" or "great work" and teams won't find enough motivation with that,' says M. C. M. Raju, a process expert in the industry. 'In my younger days, it would require very high levels of quality at work to receive an appreciation from management. These days associates demand appreciation for each and everything,' he adds.

'It is sometimes uncomfortable to provide tough feedback and have difficult conversations with the team for fear of losing them out. However, as a manager it is important to constantly sense the potential and keep raising the bar. Associates may not always know their own potential and giving them new challenges and helping them succeed with those is something I try to practise with my team,' says Karunakar Cheemarla, an engagement manager from a large organization.

DIFFICULTIES IN LEARNING

Individuals with end-to-end knowledge are in demand in organizations. They are called upon for key decisions, to fix critical problems and make right design decisions. Having such individuals is efficient for any organization as they avoid the need to run to multiple parties to achieve the same result and bring in a lot of organizational context (tacit knowledge of what is appropriate or inappropriate). And reaching this level of excellence is not an easy task.

'Gaining end-to-end knowledge (or full stack when applied to software development) would take several hands-on opportunities, complex problems, focused learning and experimentation and a heavy dose of failures too. But most importantly, one cannot settle down with one or two areas and start to get comfortable. And to be able to move to other areas, one needs to continuously train and prepare others. And all of this is tough work and needs a lot of commitment and conviction,' says Jagdeep Soni, a good friend, full stack expert and great mentor to several associates.

Teaching is an essential aspect of becoming such an end-to-end knowledgeable person.

BENEFITS OF TEACHING

During my first project in the organization, there was an expert who was assigned to a group of us (trainees) to help us work on our tasks. We would pester him with questions non-stop, and on top of that, he would still do a round occasionally and before leaving home from work to check if we needed any help. One of us asked him as to why is he willing to take on such a pain continuously in addition to doing his own work, to which he said, 'Questions from fresh minds are priceless; you have no idea how much all of you have contributed to my deep learning of the subject.'

#GameofDrones

AS AN INDIVIDUAL (BEING THE WOOD)

- I tend to get into anything which provides visibility; hence, my learning is also compliance- and need-driven.
- I do not take feedback on how much learning is enough in any given area. I have my own ways.
- My field of work is new, and not many can do what I can, so I get easy appreciations and I enjoy that. I think I can do more, but there is no need.
- I am constantly restless about what I should learn; I don't have an appreciation of what I know (I don't really know).
- I hate incremental learning and would like to get into a new area and just make it big.

- I do not take part in learning initiatives in the team or company; there isn't enough recognition for such things anyway.

AS A LEADER

- I am a manager, and I don't need to know the technical details of what my team is doing. I have delegated that fully to my SMEs.
- I push the team to be compliant on all learning expectations from my company, but I don't check their real learning.
- I am all for appreciation; usually it is a chain mail—someone starts it and we all appreciate each other; sometimes I don't know what has been done.
- I have so many super stars in the team who I have appreciated so many times, but we still have so many concerns from the customer/management.

Now discover and evaluate each roadblock. Think of it as a real drone and see how it is doing. Be honest and review how well you are flying it.

- ☐ **Fully autonomous flight**
- ☐ **Guided flights**
- ☐ **Irregular flight path**
- ☐ **Unwilling to take off**

#KeyResonatingActions

AS AN INDIVIDUAL

- Pick the area of work (as much as you can) which interests you, and learning can be natural and effective.

- Look for an expert, either within your team or outside, who can assist you with grading your learning reasonably.
- Be persistent with taking feedback (from the identified experts of mentors).
- Don't settle with easy appreciations; if you have the ability to do more, you have the opportunity to push the boundary, do it!
- Keenly learn the context of the business environment, beyond technical or field skills.
- Participate in training; learning gets reinforced with teaching.

AS A LEADER

- 'Learning ability and opportunity' of the team has got to be one of the focus items.
- Provide contrast to the team by making them interact with experts from other teams or outside; this will help them better appreciate (or invest in) their work.
- Invest yourself in an active learning programme all the time. This will pass a more emphatic message to the team than any amount of messaging on the importance of continuous learning.
- Identify the specialists in the team, provide them specific appreciation of their specialty and get them to share their experiences with the others.
- Have cross-team meet-ups where good performers can get more visibility for their efforts and zeal.
- Have a learning forum at regular intervals where senior associates of the team can announce what they have learnt new during that period of time.

- Constantly sense the 'level of ease' with which individuals are performing and provide them more challenging assignments to match up to their skill level.

#StickyNoteWorthy

Every act of conscious learning requires the willingness to suffer an injury to one's self-esteem. That is why young children, before they are aware of their own self-importance, learn so easily.

Thomas Szasz

Workplaces are contagious. Whether we like it or not, something is continuously getting spread. Whether it is apathy, competition, culture to work in a silo (or) if it is empathy, sharing values, enabling each other and building upon each other's wisdom is a choice the teams and leadership must make consciously. Engaging in an effort of learning the right elements in a spirit of teaching (sharing) is the best way to build an inspiring workplace which constantly strives to bring smiles to the customers.

Creating a zeal of learning in the team is winning the battle by 50 per cent; the team would ensure that the rest 50 per cent is won with ease. This can best be achieved with persistent focus and creative nudging of everyone in the team regardless of role or hierarchy. And what can be more impactful than the leader of the group taking it on from the front and leading by example!

23

TRUE POWER

Identity vs Reputation

It was the autumn session of the university. Thirty-five young and sharp minds were assembled in their first class of the management programme for business administration. The enthusiasm was visible, and every student was radiating a sense of achievement and victory in life. And why not, they had tried very hard to crack the entrance examination, followed by rigorous rounds of interviews, group discussions and role-plays. It was a dream university to get into, and these few had done it. 'We are set for life!' they thought as they interacted with each other.

Professor Phillip walked into the class to start the proceedings for the programme. 'Mmm … hmmm', he said as he was hit by a thunderous reception and a resounding greeting from the class. 'I would like to see you carry this spirit until the very last day of this programme,' he said with a mild smile, 'Settle down now please.'

'Today, we will keep the session lighter. I will be journeying with you for the next two years and will be your guide in the learning programme. To be precise, I will discuss with you the subjects of business ethics, managerial economics and applied statistics. I hold a PhD in managerial economics, statistics and accounting,' he told the class. There was rapt attention as if the students were exposed to divine music. 'I take it that you are impressed with my company, very good. Let us get to know each other a little bit, shall we?' said the professor.

'It has been my dream to enrol with this institution for the MBA programme, professor, and get to sit in your class. This is a dream come true,' said Peter. 'I have a plan for my life, and an MBA with a prestigious institution such as this is a step forward; I am happy to be here,' said Angela. As the students went through sharing their background and their expectations from the programme, Professor Phillip gently smiled and tried to absorb as much as he could.

'I see an MBA as a step towards moving to an executive role,' said Tyron. 'And why do you want to be an executive my friend?' asked the professor. 'To be completely honest with you, I think it gives me power. It gives me authority. People will just listen to what I say. I would love to get things done and nothing better than being in an executive authority to do so. Of course, I am smart and that's why I am here,' Tyron spoke honestly. The professor paused for a moment and the class keenly watched his face.

Tyron was beginning to get uncomfortable with the silence when the professor said, 'I like your honest opinion and the way you have expressed it. I encourage all of you to be direct and speak out your mind. I can assist you only when I know where I should, and we can help each other out by being open. Now coming back to what Tyron said…,' he paused again to adjust his spectacles which were beginning to dance down his hawk like nose.

'How many of you believe that doing an MBA is a road to an executive position?' A few hands went up hesitatingly. 'How many of you think that being an executive gives you the power to execute?' Fewer hands this time. 'And how many of you think that people will listen to your authority, to whatever you say?' This time, Tyron was alone with his hand half raised. 'Well, I must reconsider professorship and look for a position of power myself, shouldn't I?' he chuckled, and the class responded with an uncomfortable laughter. 'I am glad that we are discussing this topic upfront, and I will revisit this several, no, much more than that, times during the programme. For today, let us play a small game.'

'Tyron, you are the executive "with a simple order", and we will come to that later. I want the rest of the class to split into two groups. Each group please move to one corner of the room,' said the professor with his hand leaning on the large mahogany desk towards the front of the classroom. 'I will speak with our executive here and will then come to each of the groups with a message "about him" and then we will play the game.' Saying so he first went to Tyron. 'You will tell each group, after I have spoken to them, to execute an order, that of trying to move this table here. Please wait for my signal before you go to them and make the most respectful but assertive directive to each of the groups.' Tyron saw that the professor then went to the two groups one by one and spent few minutes telling them something. He noticed that a few members from each group gave him a few glances as they heard the professor.

'OK, Tyron, you are to give an order which your teams will execute. First, please go to the group to the right and tell them what they should do for you,' said Phillip. With the professor following closely, Tyron walked up to the group on the right side of the room and said, 'It is very important for us as a company to move things forward. I would like to work with a team which has discipline and can execute the directives of their executives. With that, I would like you to trust me and move that table over there.'

'Impressive!' said Phillip, and Tyron broadened his shoulders in confidence. The other group which was a few yards away on the other side of the room was watching keenly as to what was happening. The group which received the order reluctantly went to the table and gathered around looking at it. After a while, one of them tried to lean on it with a forward bend and motioned the others to do the same with a smirk. Others followed suit. 'It definitely looks like they are trying to do what you told them to do,' whispered Phillip to Tyron. 'But this is not fair! The group is not playing to the rules, professor,' said Tyron with his confidence fading away. 'Please wait for it and then repeat your orders to the second group.' After few minutes, the professor motioned to the first group to return to their seats.

Tyron then walked over to the second group and gave them exactly the same orders. The group rose instantly and went to the table. They observed the table for a while as a group as if to understand the difficulty of the task. In a few minutes collectively, they managed to push the huge table by a few inches, making a screeching noise. 'Bravo!' said Phillip, and Tyron looked at the other group with a sense of 'See? That's how it's done' on his face.

The professor thanked the second group and asked them to settle down. 'This was an extremely simple and elementary exercise of getting your teams to execute for you—to move a table. As executives, you will have power, but that is realized only when it is allowed to be exercised by those who will work for you, nay, work with you.

Tyron, I was being *your reputation*—"everything which you are perceived to stand out for". To the first group I told this—"Tyron is an executive in power. If you do not follow his orders, he may fire you all and all of you need your job very much. However, conventionally his actions are not clear and he may tell you to do something which is probably important for the company, but the relevance is not understood by you. His past actions did not follow through with a clarification of how they have brought value for the company, to the employees and to the community. However, not following his orders is not an option." And to the second group I told the following: "Tyron has built this company for you. Everything he says and does has inherently in it an aspect of growth beyond himself. His actions in the past have always had a larger purpose behind them, which significantly made a difference to his employees and the community. He may not fire you if you do not do what he says but doing so will ensure that collectively you have moved one step further as a team."'

'I am also glad that the second group did want to move further as a team and trusted their executive. You have a good team, Tyron,' Phillip winked at him as Tyron smiled in acknowledgement.

'So, you see, true power to execute is realized by the effectiveness of execution, and it is only made possible by the trust and faith placed by the ecosystem. Through the course you will learn several techniques which will help you get to the right decisions—"on which tables to move and which ones to let be". But connecting with the ones around and developing the reach to get things done, you must build yourself. And if I might add, for that you do not have to wait to become an "executive,"' concluded Phillip with a warm smile.

#WorkplaceWhispers

The classic gap between identity (my perception about myself) and reputation (what others think about me) is not just applicable for those in leadership roles but also for anyone in general. Bridging this gap to align it with reality by either (a) correcting perceptions about self or (b) correcting the perception of others is an endeavour of mindfulness, self-awareness, sensing/seeking feedback, willingness to change and persistence with actions.

REPUTATION AND OPPORTUNITY (INDIVIDUAL)

Associates go through a lot of frustration when their perception of self does not match with their reputation, leading to an opportunity loss. Consider this not-so-uncommon discussion between an aspiring associate (AA) and his manager (M):

AA: 'I have been leading this module for several years now. I think I have bagged the experience and skills needed to move to the next level and take up project lead role for all the modules.'

M: 'Indeed, you have delivered well in this module, but as a skilled individual contributor. You have also provided support to the newcomers and others in the module, and naturally we have looked up to you for updates. But you will have to work on your interpersonal skills, develop project management skills and understand what happens beyond your module/develop an end-to-end view. Without this, we will be setting you up for failure by pushing you to the next level.'

As a manager, it will help if the associate got constant interim feedback so that this gap does not arise in the first place.

POWER VS REPUTATION (LEADER)

Is reputation important when there is tremendous power to influence and drive alignment? The answer to this lies in the belief system of the leader. Depending on how a leader gets positioned in his role of leadership (coming from outside with credentials, someone who grew with the team, someone who built the team and so on) and what baggage he already carries, building a good reputation can be a long-term affair at best, to being an impossible feat at worst. But if the leader does not recognize the need for building a good reputation in the first place, then it can be an ever-elusive affair.

LET'S MEET AND GREET

Although gone are the days where the executives used to reach out to their employees with hand-written memos, and such traditional means of communication, and much swifter real-time channels have appeared, the problem of 'genuinely connecting' with the teams remains a hard one to tackle on a continuous basis. And without a good connect, reputation remains at the mercy of individual assumptions and perceptions. But connecting with people is sometimes confused with calling multiple meet-ups and overloading the team with information. If not done effectively, teams would quickly lose interest, and this would end up being a compliance norm.

FOLLOWING THROUGH...

As much as it is important to explain 'why' a request/directive is being made, it is equally important to follow through and update the team on the logical next steps—for instance, conducting surveys, asking for feedback, soliciting information or getting the team to work on a laborious task. Post this activity, if the management does not come back to explain what was done with this information, and more importantly how it would impact the ways of working of the team, next time around there will be much feeble participation for such requests. And this will also impact the reputation of the leader.

AGENTS OF REPUTATION

All of us directly or indirectly keep contributing to this shape shifter called reputation—sometimes our own and sometimes to that of others. One should be watchful of one's dominant behaviours, usage of words and more importantly how one's team is further spreading them to the others. I am sure you empathize with the following reputation types based on dominant actions/messages:

- Messenger: 'I don't know why this is needed; boss told me to tell you this and get the work done....'

- Messengers also tend to leave a bad reputation on their managers too if they don't represent the management the right way.

- Apathetic manager: 'Do I look like I care about what you think? Just get it done.'
- Complainer: 'Things are so slow; nothing gets done here; issues, issues, issues everywhere….'
- Hierarchical manager:'You cannot talk to the senior manager directly without going through me….'
- Dependable:'She gets the job done, no matter what; she has never failed in any programme….'
- Constant learner:'One thing I have seen her do is that she never stops learning. Put her in any project, she picks up with sheer effort and determination and delivers….'

HAVING A GREAT FIRST-LEVEL TEAM

With the organization continuously expanding, it was time for moving some of the associates to a different location in Sao Paulo, which was 50 km outside the city. It was a tough decision, and for the associates it would be a nightmare to travel to this far-away place from their homes every day. Maria, head of operations for the delivery centre, got the directive from her executive to move 50 projects out of the current location, impacting at least 500 associates. She understood why the organization was pushing them to do so, but facing the team was not an easy task. The easiest thing to do was to push the blame on the executive who issued the order and complain along with the team. Instead, Maria chose to take a two-pronged approach. She took fierce fights with management to ensure that better logistics facilities were provided, and the move was done in a phased manner. She was the voice of the team and pushed the executives hard. She explained how this would impact the lives of her team and what it would mean to business. With the team, she was the face of management. She explained to the team with empathy as to how it would benefit the organization and what it would mean to all of them in the long run. She chose to shift her own work location and be with the team which was moving.

In the above narrative based on real incidents, Maria not just protected the reputation of the executive and her company in front of the team but also vice versa. Having such individuals like Maria in the team is a great way to ensure that negativity does not spread in the organization with every difficult decision which is taken.

#GameofDrones

AS AN INDIVIDUAL

- I think I am ready to do more, but my manager does not think so.
- I try to be nice with everyone and keep changing my stance easily—even at the cost of putting my manager's or other groups' reputation at stake.
- I am not mindful of my dominant behaviours—some people say I speak too fast and no one understands me.
- I try to use influence or escalation to get the job done.

AS A LEADER

- I have a hard time convincing the individuals about their potential and what more they have to learn.
- I have a feeling of insecurity not knowing what my team thinks about me.
- I am unmindful of what my team thinks; I do what I think is right.

- I prefer using my position of authority to get the job done.
- I am in an organization where role matters more than the work at hand.

Now discover and evaluate each roadblock. Think of it as a real drone and see how it is doing. Be honest and review how well you are flying it.

☐ **Fully autonomous flight**

☐ **Guided flights**

☐ **Irregular flight path**

☐ **Unwilling to take off**

#KeyResonatingActions

AS AN INDIVIDUAL

- Practise self-reflection and have a friend at work to provide critical and timely feedback.
- Constantly check what kind of dominant activities you are into and what reputation you are gathering due to those.
- Always try to carry a professional opinion (put effort to get to it) and not shift blame to someone else.
- Ask for more details when something is not understood and do not spread information which you don't yourself understand.
- Do not encourage gossip or negativity.

AS A LEADER

- Be a listening leader—team understands that not everything can be solved, but they still expect an unbiased 'ear' of their leader.

- Be a relentless leader when it comes to supporting your team (for the right reasons).
- Try to connect with different levels of the organization to understand how your messages are being translated and relayed by your first level.
- Provide as much clarity as possible while making an ask and always follow through with your promises.
- Encourage individuals to take up more ownership and empower them to do so, regardless of their official titles.

#StickyNoteWorthy

What the tongue has promised, the body must submit to.

Rex Stout

Integrity is an attribute which is constantly under check for every individual, but more so for a leader. Teams expect their leader to be a role model under every situation, and especially under difficult ones. Providing the 'why' of their job role to every individual to the team, the 'why' of every ask made and reminding the 'why' of the organization are great ways to build a good reputation and also connecting with the team. And here lies the true power to execute and get things done.

I would like to congratulate you, the conscientious manager, for acknowledging the importance of workplace ethics and investing your time in reading through the narratives of this book. As we read through each chapter and reflected together, we saw three underlying themes staying rooted on the canvas on which all the narratives unfolded:

- Every voice is important, and every individual carries a potentiality which can be nurtured into a wonderful opportunity for the group or organization which he/she belongs to.
- Being conscientious is difficult, but the struggle is very gratifying.
- It is *easier to adhere to great practices if done together as a team.*

And towards the third theme above, it is important that every individual transmits positive narratives in the organization consciously. It is unfortunate that usually the negative stories travel faster than the positive ones, and it is for individuals like you, with purpose and drive, to reverse this trend.

Workplace ethics backed by a strong value system have always been important. In the wake of new-age technologies and rapidly changing demands, the workplace is only going to get:

- increasingly virtual.
- complex and diverse.
- vast *in obvious and subtle ways—enveloping large-scale ecosystems.*

Although several technology controls are also going to be put in place to integrate security and trust in the transactions (via technologies of blockchain and AI-based cybersecurity), the reliance on an 'ennobled individual', enriched by a strong value system and ethics, is going to be pivotal, more than anything else. I hope that this book makes a small and bold step towards enabling that ideal.

In conclusion, I would like to make an appeal to every reader of the book to boldly continue on their journey of conscientiousness and not give up. My hope is that the narratives in the book served as a reflecting mirror or a sounding board to both affirm some of the good practices you have been following and provide suggestions to arrive at new ones. Discussing some of these along with your teams is a great way to face the scruples of the workplace and arriving at genuine KRAs. I encourage you to revisit these narratives often for inspiration and making necessary course corrections as your context changes. I wish you all the best in your endeavours of making a difference to yourself and others.

Burg, Bob, and John Mann David. *The Go-giver Leader: A Little Story about What Matters Most in Business*. London: Penguin Random House, 2016.

Christensen, Clayton M., Taddy Hall, Karen Dillon, and David S. Duncan. *Competing against Luck: The Story of Innovation and Customer Choice*. New York, NY: Harper Business, 2016.

Gallo, Carmine. *The Storyteller's Secret: How TED Speakers and Inspirational Leaders Turn Their Passion into Performance*. London: Macmillan Publishers, 2016.

Gene, Kim, Kevin Behr, and George Spafford. *The Phoenix Project: A Novel about IT DevOps, and Helping Your Business Win*. Portland, OR: IT Revolution Press, 2013.

McCabe, Dr Andrew Aloysius. *The Gifted One: The Journey Begins*. Bloomington, IN: Balboa Press, 2011.

Ramakrishna, Prayaga. *Rules to Rulers: Eternal Wisdom from Epics*. Translated from Telugu by D. Rangarao. Hyderabad: Prayaga Ramakrishna, 2010.

ABOUT THE AUTHOR

Phani Medicharla is an avid writer (storyteller and poet) in the world of technology consulting. He lives in Stockholm, Sweden, and works as a relationship manager, heading a large technology function for TCS. Phani has international exposure working in geographies such as—APAC, North America and Europe—working with several global customers in multiple business domains. In his long career, he has performed several roles, led diverse multicultural teams and interacted with great leaders.

Phani is a keen observer of the day-to-day workplace interactions and an advocate of experiential learning. He strongly believes that appreciating diversity and inspiring the latent potential in each other with empathy, are the only ways to succeed collectively and deliver sustainable value in any profession. What motivates him the most in the workplace is the opportunity to cultivate a cheerful and embracing environment which promotes holistic growth for everyone. A vegan by choice, Phani believes in a higher purpose for life and that technology/business should be conducted with an 'ethics first' attitude.

To share your experiences and adventures of conscientiousness, please connect with Phani at phani@theconscientiousmanager.com.